Leadership

moment

brought to you by EQUIP

This book is a collection of the numerous works of JOHN C. MAXWELL

As Heard On

Leadership Moment, the daily radio ministry of EQUIP.

John C. Maxwell, Content Provider
EQUIP Founder

John Hull, Executive Editor and Host
President and CEO of EQUIP

Tom Atema, Executive Producer
EQUIP Vice President of International
Ministries and Strategic Partnerships

Daniel Walters, Producer
Communications Technology Coordinator for
EQUIP and Leadership Moment

Distributed by Walter F. Bennett Communications
Philadelphia, Pennsylvania

*Leadership Moments, 365 Inspirational Thoughts for the
Leader's Year*
Copyright © 2008 by EQUIP
All Rights Reserved

Published by EQUIP
12000 Findley Road, Suite 150
Johns Creek, GA 30097

Cover and interior design by Leigh Germy Creative
Design.
Printed by Bethany Press International.

ISBN: 978-1-931132-18-3

Scripture quotations are taken from the *Holy Bible*, New
International Version®. NIV®.

Books by Dr. John C. Maxwell

RELATIONSHIPS

Be a Person of Influence · Becoming a Person of Influence · Relationships 101
The Power of Influence · The Power of Partnership in the Church · The Treasure
of a Friend · Ethics 101 · Winning with People · 25 Ways to Win with People

EQUIPPING

Developing the Leaders Around You · Equipping 101 · The 17 Indisputable Laws
of Teamwork · The 17 Essential Qualities of a Team Player · Partners in Prayer
You Road Map for Success · Success One Day at a Time · Today Matters
Talent is Never Enough

ATTITUDE

Be All You Can Be · Failing Forward · The Power of Thinking Big · Living at the
Next Level · Think on These Things · The Winning Attitude · Your Bridge to a
Better Future · The Power of Attitude · Attitude 101 · Thinking for a Change
The Difference Maker · The Journey from Success to Significance

LEADERSHIP

The 21 Indispensable Qualities of a Leader · Revised and Updated 10th Anniversary
Edition of The 21 Irrefutable Laws of Leadership · The 21 Most Powerful Minutes
in a Leader's Day · Developing the Leader Within You · Leadership 101
Leadership Promises for Every Day · The 360 Degree Leader · The Right to Lead
The Power of Leadership · Leadership Gold · Go for the Gold

A New Year is upon us!

For some of us, there is excitement and anticipation. Yet for others, you're nervous and afraid. Fear doesn't respect anyone. It touches all ages. It's acquainted with every walk of life. Fear can be destructive and paralyzing. Fear is torment.

Before David was a king, he was a fugitive—living on the run. And in the weariness of the chase, he grew fearful. But David paused from the chase long enough to remind himself in Psalm 34, that God always protects and God always provides.

Today, as you face the New Year, remember the God of David is your God too. He will protect. He will provide.

I have some really great news as this new year begins.

No man or woman who trusts in Jesus Christ needs to be afraid of death. Jesus said, *"Because I live, you shall live also."* At Christmas we celebrate because God became man in order to deliver us from death.

At New Year's, we celebrate that we've been given a new life and new opportunities to live for Christ. David said in Psalm 34, *"I sought the Lord and he delivered me from all my fears."*

As you face another new year, don't face it with fear. Face it in confidence because Jesus Christ has come. And because he's come, we need not fear.

Low Road vs. High Road

The low road is where we treat others worse than they treat us. The middle road, well that's where we treat others the same as they treat us. The high road though, that's where you treat others better than they treat you.

The low road is the easiest road but its destination is sorrow. The low road damages relationships, and alienates others from us.

And while the middle road may not drive people away, it may not attract them to you either.

The high road is the only road for the Christian leader. It requires COURAGE and it requires some TALENT, actually putting some life skills to work.

When the high road is your road, you turn the other cheek, you stay above the fray and do your best to glorify God.

Today, be exceptional. Choose to take the high road.

Adversity is a Partner of Progress

Advice columnist Ann Landers wrote, "If I were asked to give what I consider the single most useful piece of advice for all humanity, it would be this: Expect trouble as an inevitable part of life and when it comes, hold your head high, look it squarely in the eye and say, "I will be bigger than you. You cannot defeat me."

The Scripture echoes this idea when it speaks of rain falling on the just and the unjust and we shouldn't think it strange when difficult times come upon us. After all, a world cursed with sin puts us to the test every day.

But here's the good news... adversity is always a partner of progress. Anytime we want to move forward, obstacles and problems will get in the way. Instead of praying, "God get me out of this," how about praying, "What do you want me to get out of this?"

That's the prayer of a leader.

Today and in all of life's difficulties, make this your prayer.

JAN
Facing Obstacles

The famous novelist, H.G. Wells once asked, "What on earth would a man do with himself if something didn't stand in his way?"

Every leader knows that there always seems to be something standing in the way of progress. Problems, obstacles, predicaments, critics... the list can go on and on.

Today, why not see adversity as your friend?

You see, you can count it a joy today when obstacles are in the path. That obstacle will teach you about your strengths and weaknesses. That obstacle will shape you.

The people who made the greatest marks on history are those who, when faced with obstacles, stayed the course, met the challenge and rose to the occasion.

If you're facing an obstacle—keep facing it! In time, with God's help, you'll overcome.

Be Courageous!

During the Great Depression, Thomas Edison delivered his last public message.

He said, "My message to you is this: Be courageous! I have lived a long time. I have seen history repeat itself again and again. Be as brave as your fathers before you. Have faith. Go forward!"

Edison knew that when we experience fear, we must be willing to move forward.

Now that is an individual decision. Courage starts internally before it's displayed externally. We must first win the battle within ourselves.

Years ago, when reading an editor's request for readers to respond to the question, "What's wrong with the world?" G.K. Chesterton wrote this reply, "Dear Sir, I am. Yours Sincerely, G.K. Chesterton."

Today - take responsibility, be courageous, stand strong, and move forward!

Be Fully Engaged in Life

It's kind of sad when people allow themselves to get in a rut and never climb out. They often miss the best that life has to offer.

In contrast, teachable people are fully engaged in life. They get excited about things. They are interested in discovery, discussion, application and growth. There is a definite relationship between passion and potential.

One philosopher coined it this way: *"Never let a day pass without looking at some perfect work of art, hearing some great piece of music and reading, in part, some great book."*

Great advice! The more engaged you are, the more interesting life will be. The more you learn and explore, the greater your potential for growth.

Don't let today pass you by! Listen, read, see–do something that will help you to grow and engage.

The Roman scholar Cato started to learn Greek when he was more than 80 years old.

When asked why he wanted to start something so difficult at such a late age, he said, "It's the earliest age I have left." Unlike Cato, too many people regard learning as an event instead of a process.

I read recently that only one-third of all adults read an entire book after their last graduation. Why? I think it's that they see learning as a period of life, not as a way of life. Learning is important. Even in the life of Jesus, Luke 2:52 says, that "he grew in wisdom and stature, in favor with God and with man."

Leaders are learners.

It doesn't matter if you're past 80 like Cato or haven't yet started high school. Learning should be an on-going part of your life!

Make it your mission today to learn something new.

A key step in overcoming pride is recognizing that it is a problem since those who are bound by it are often unaware of it. To defeat pride, we need to embrace humility, and few desire that.

C.S. Lewis remarked, "If any would like to acquire humility, I can, I think, tell them the first step. The first step is to realize that one is proud. If you think you are not conceited, you are very conceited indeed."

People have a natural tendency to believe that they are indispensable, that the world will stop and take notice if anything happens to them. But that's just not reality.

Today, do your best to remember that no one is indispensible.

Words have power.

Turn on any news channel or talk show and you will hear of some recent feud in Hollywood, politics or the business world. Slander, gossip, rumors and lies seem to be a rampant part of our society today.

Words really do matter. They have the power to heal or the power to hurt. Words can build people up... or tear people down.

The BEST leaders understand that their words set the tone for this morning's meeting at the office and tonight's conversation around the family dinner table.

Mark Twain once said that the difference between finding the right word and the "almost" right word is as big a difference between lightning and a lightning bug!

Good leaders understand that choosing the right words at the right time empower and bless those who follow.

Today, be especially aware of the power of your words. Not only to watch what you say, but also to affirm and encourage those around you!

The press called it "The Missouri Miracle." The story that caught the nation's attention, reported that two abducted and missing boys near St. Louis had been found!

The boys were discovered, thanks in large measure to the work of two uniform police officers who were alert to the case.

This story should remind all of us of the noble work law enforcement officers perform every day all across this land. These community leaders deserve our respect and need our prayers.

They are peace officers- and because they are willing to patrol our streets and keep order in our communities, you and I get the opportunity to lead our families in a safer environment so that they might become better citizens... better leaders!

Today, say a special prayer for your community's peace officers.

Connect-ability

A trait of a strong leader is "*connect-ability.*"

Our Biblical example is Nehemiah–the construction of the wall followed his connection with the people.

Nehemiah connected with the hearts of his volunteers before asking them to sacrifice their time and energy. Nehemiah appealed to their sense of dignity, identity and responsibility.

You see, it is always the leader's responsibility to connect to the people, not the people with the leader. In order to connect, the leader has to be a good listener; listening to where the people are and to find the connection point, then move the people forward.

Take time out of your day to truly connect to those around you. Really listen.

It is important for any leader to be *creative*.

There is no question that we live in a complex world with complex issues. The world is changing daily and leaders have to be able to adapt to the changing times with creativity!

Our biblical example here is Ezekiel. You remember the story. Israel was acting like a stubborn mule and wouldn't listen to the prophet's words. Ezekiel had to adapt to the needs of his audience.

Many times a leader has to go out on a limb and be willing to try something different to solve a problem or meet a need. Leaders think outside the box because leadership is all about managing change.

Take a moment today to brainstorm and reflect upon how you can be an outside-of-the-box leader!

Communication, Part 1

As we learn to be betters leaders, one trait we must strive for is an ability to *communicate*.

I'm not talking about making great sound bites. I'm talking about being able to communicate the truth of the situation so the people can understand the problem and the solution.

Our Biblical example for this trait is Samuel–Mr. Communicator. Everyone listened to him.

Samuel not only demonstrated credibility with his passion and his life, he lived out what he said. He spoke the truth no matter how hard it was. He overflowed with honest content, edifying and teaching others.

Samuel always made sure that his words and his life matched up. He spoke truth, but also lived it out by example.

Today, make it your mission to communicate truth through words AND actions!

Like all good communications, Samuel also kept his message simple. He was straight forward, concise and to the point.

A great communicator seeks a response. Samuel's communication was filled with purpose. When he finished he urged people to do their part, giving them clear direction and hope for their future

Great communicators and leaders touch the heart before the head (the mind).

Be a straight-forward communicator!

Credibility

A must-have leadership trait is *credibility*.

Colin Powell said, "Leadership is a combination of strategy and character–if you must be without one, drop the strategy."

You see, character + competence = credibility.

For a leader to lead, he/she must have followers. And to have followers, a leader must have credibility.

Many leaders talk the talk, but don't walk the walk. Others pass the integrity test but fail to lead effectively. People may like them as a friend, but won't follow them as a leader. There is a big difference in the two.

David is our Biblical example here. David succeeded because he had hands and a heart–every leader then and now needs both. A leader must have this combination–to not have these in balance will lead to failure.

Today, make sure that your creed and your deeds are the same!

A leader today must have *courage*.

Courage is the commitment to do the right thing in the face of possible criticism.

Courage is the first essential quality for effective leaders. Leaders initiate and take a stand even when no one else is traveling with them.

In the Bible, Paul encouraged Timothy to take courage and do what was right in difficult times.

Leaders must work daily on the qualities of character and integrity. A leader has to care more about their integrity than their image. And that means resisting the temptation to abuse their power and position in their personal life–for the personal life is reflected in their public life.

Courage is taking a position even when you know it might cost you something.

Today, be a courageous leader. Stand strong in the face of difficult decisions!

A leader today needs to have *conviction*.

Let me ask you a question: Do leaders always love and care for people, regardless of who they are? Yes–certainly.

Hosea is our biblical example of a leader who showed conviction by modeling unconditional love.

Leaders are to love and care for everyone. This however, doesn't mean they disregard their convictions. They respond with grace, but never drift from their convictions. They speak gently, but with focus. With conviction we cling to the course we are to travel.

Leaders always act from their principles; empowering others even when it is hard.

Today, be a leader of conviction. Work out of grace.

More than ever leaders today need to have *charisma*.

Charisma has been defined as a magnetic personal attraction that draws others to the leader. Charisma is the quality that makes people want to listen to you and support you. It is the ability to inspire one to be and do more than they thought possible.

Now in the Bible both Ahab and Jezebel felt no incentive to develop charisma because they thought their positions allowed them to use people and manipulate them. They were selfish and cunning to get what they wanted.

Good leaders understand the value of pouring their life into others, and that is what gives you charisma!

How will you pour into others today?

To build charisma, you need to be others-minded.

Leaders who think of others and their concerns before thinking of themselves quickly develop charisma.

In the Bible, leaders who were more concerned about the citizens than themselves always prospered and the nation of Israel was blessed by them.

Pride is what will keep you from having charisma. So will insecurity. Only secure leaders can provide a secure atmosphere.

Charisma will get you an audience—but only character will keep the audience.

Today, will you provide a secure atmosphere?

A leader must be *competent*.

A competent leader is one whose life is built on a process!

Competence rarely happens overnight! Even the great Joshua had to be prepared over many years to handle the enormous task given him.

By the time he died, competence could have been Joshua's middle name.

Consider this:

- God used Joshua over the course of two generations.
- God trusted Joshua to lead the military campaigns from the wilderness to Canaan, the Promised Land.
- God used Joshua to accompany Moses up Mount Sinai.
- God replaced Moses with Joshua, having served 40 years as an understudy. Joshua's competence grew through Moses' tutoring and his own observations.

Are you making the right choices today to help build your competence for what God has planned?

Common Sense, Part 1

A leader needs to possess *common sense*–a willingness to listen to the voice of reason when it might not make sense.

We might call this discernment because leaders read the situation before they lead!

God handles each circumstance based on His assessment of the individual situation. In Ezekiel 18, God reminds us to use discernment in each situation we face.

Don't lump everyone together; size everyone up one at a time. Respond correctly to each situation.

Give every single person and situation a chance. You may be surprised.

Common sense is that gut feeling.

A leader has to analyze past successes–to identify root issues of success and failure. Leaders can fall into such a rut that they begin to stereotype everyone. Let each team member be an individual and discern what is right for them without the baggage of others.

A leader has to listen to their gut. Try to recall times when your intuition "spoke" to you correctly. Get data, but go beyond mere information to your heart's sense of what is the right thing.

Pray to God for discernment and intuition on how to handle each situation every day.

A leader needs to have the *correct team*.

Leaders are not supposed to do all the work! What they are supposed to do is assemble a team who buys into the vision with passion. Leaders build teams by effectively using the talent of each team member. Great teams use every gift and enjoy both unity of vision and the diversity of gifts.

The people around the leader will either make or break the leader! The biggest potential problem a leader has is his or her ego which can cause the leader to do dumb things.

Having the right people around the leader will help the leader set the right priorities. And having the right priorities will help the leader choose the right people.

Are the right people on your team? Are your priorities and motives upon your team empowering them or breaking them?

Leadership comes with a cost.

When you read the story of Hosea in the Bible, it can be a very painful thing. Here's a man with a wayward wife who is stubbornly clinging to the wrong kinds of relationships. His marriage is in trouble and yet he sensed a great call of God in his life to communicate the truth of God in society.

He was a leader in conflict.

Hosea was also a leader who needed to stay close to God. And staying close to God served as a reminder to him that he belonged to God, that God was in control of his life and that while walking with the Lord is a blessing–as a leader, it also carries with it a burden.

Are you in a conflict today? Stay close to God and He will guide you.

Leaders Set the Tone for Followers

God calls leaders to live on a higher level than followers.

Hosea the prophet was told by God to go and reconcile with his wife who was involving herself in some very inappropriate relationships. When God tells Hosea to pursue reconciliation, He says to act with love rather than take revenge.

That's a higher level of living than is required of followers. Followers tend to want to act out, create drama, be a victim, and get even. But leaders are called to be examples and set the tone for followers, to take the high road, staying focused on obedience to God and operate out of principle rather than reaction.

It is a daily choice whether or not to be a follower or hold firm to integrity as a leader. Who will you be today?

You cannot be a true leader without basic integrity.

Leaders who cannot be trusted with basic integrity will surely suffer not only God's anger, but the anger of their followers too.

Back in the Old Testament book of Hosea, the leaders there established boundary stones which helped to bring definition to a plot of land.

As the Biblical story unfolds, Israel's leaders moved the boundary stones–and that was a "no-no" in the eyes of God and the people. By doing so, they raised questions about their values and their honesty.

When leaders establish their own boundary stones to people, they better make sure they have a good sound reason to move them. Wavering, changing promises, not keeping your word, will cost you as a leader in your integrity and it will raise a lot of questions of trust.

Today, are you holding firm to integrity?

JAN
DAY 28

The Art of Confrontation

It's true, not many people like to confront.

But those who are good at it, for the right reasons, have really turned it into an art form. And here are some of the guidelines that folks who confront well work by:

- They express the kind of relationship they wish they had with the offending person
- They clarify what the root problem is
- They point to values and priorities
- They remind the offending person of the consequences of their bad behavior.

All good confrontation ends with the hope of reconciliation and not excommunication.

If you're facing a confrontation, learn from folks who know how to confront well…and for the glory of God and the betterment of the person you're confronting, always treat them as you would want to be treated.

Do you have a conflict with someone that needs to be addressed? Remember to confront out of prayerful discernment and love.

Our mission as leaders should always be to give the glory back to God.

If a successful leader isn't careful, one of the missing pieces in their leadership style, as success grows, is humility. It's often easy to forget the prosperity and blessing which comes from God and begin to act as if all those good things came because you, the leader, are God's gift to the solar system.

Well, only Jesus was God's gift on the interplanetary level. You and I are just fallen souls who have experienced grace—the grace of God. We err as leaders when we assume that we are the source of blessing and success. Wise leaders make good decisions, but realize that the outcome remains in God's hands. Leaders merely manage what God already knows.

Let this be an encouragement to you today, God is in full control and He is worthy of our praise!

The best leaders are relevant.

They understand the times they live in and find words to help communicate how to live in those times with power and influence. They are relevant.

Being relevant means using temporal surroundings to say what is timeless. The prophet Joel used the current events of his time to share timeless truth. When he saw Israel in freefall, he grabbed the public's attention by illustrating the fact that God was going to judge the nation. Now while what he said wasn't popular, it sure was clear. Joel used word pictures, kept to his message and made sure his word pictures and messages were in concert.

Answering questions today that people are asking is the job of a leader. It's called relevance. It's what Joel was then, and what leaders should be now.

Are you a relevant leader? Use examples to better portray your message, but keep your message the same and clear.

My friend Tim Elmore says that "Intuition is like a head start in a race; you can beat the fastest runner in the world with a big enough head start."

The prophet Joel provides a head start in his leadership in Israel because he had great intuition as to what God was doing and compared that to the people's needs. Joel stayed ahead of the curve and the crowd in a very wise and discerning manner.

Now how's your intuition, my friend? Can you sense and feel the way things are going, what people are thinking, how situations are progressing? If you can, you've gotten a head start and could very well win the race of influencing others for God and for good.

Take time out of your day to reflect upon your intuitive progress.

Invitation to Lead

The call to leadership is a consistent pattern in the Bible.

It began with Adam, when God told him to take dominion over the earth. And even after man fell into sin, God continued to invite him to take part in His work ... to lead others as we follow Him.

When God decided to birth a nation of His own, He didn't call upon the masses. He groomed one man... Abraham. When the Israelites escaped the chains of slavery, God raised up Moses to lead them to the brink of the Promised Land... and Joshua to lead them home.

In your family, your church, your world... every time God wants to do something great, He calls a leader to step forward.

Today, listen for what He is calling you to be and to do.

Who can stand up under the purification process of God? Who can remain unchanged through the fire of God? These are the questions Isaiah asks and answers in chapter 33 of his prophecy. Here are the traits of a few people who can stand up in times of crisis.

Integrity... the leader's life matches his words.

Justice... the leader rejects dishonest gain.

Conviction... the leader's values won't allow him or her to accept bribes.

Purity... The leader disciplines his or her mind to remain clean.

Right now, consider these four attributes and decipher which one you may need some growth in. Make it your prayer today for God to strengthen you with His fire.

You are what you reproduce.

When David fled from Saul, he attracted several men who eventually became like him. In doing so, he proved this about leadership... what you are, is what you reproduce.

Long before David was a king, David was a leader. He attracted men even without pursuing them. He instilled loyalty in them without trying to get it. He transformed them without judging them. He didn't send them into battle alone. He fought alongside them and turned them into winners.

David attracted men like himself–souls in distress–and reproduced men like himself–warriors and conquerors.

So can you.

When you think of servant-hood, what comes to mind?

You know, being a servant is not about position or skill. Attitude is far more important than aptitude. Bad leaders are easy to spot. They value status ahead of service and rights ahead of responsibilities.

True servant leaders look for ways to serve others, not themselves. They sacrifice their own agenda. They care nothing about personal advancement and they're motivated by genuine, Christ-like love.

Do you want to be a leader today? If so, remember that the extent of your influence depends on the depth of your concern for those around you. That's why it is so important for leaders to be willing to serve.

Be Careful Where You Get Your Counsel

Where are you receiving your counsel?

Leaders, take note of the instruction found in the first Psalm. It is a contrast between the righteous and the wicked. And the difference in the two is where they get their counsel.

Observe the downward progression of the foolish leader. He looks for the wrong counsel, he listens to the wrong voices, and finally, he links himself to the wrong inner circle.

Contrast this with the wise leader who daily meditates on God's Word. Sure, he seeks counsel from other members of the Body of Christ. But he weighs and measures it against the infallible, undeniable truth of Scripture, and then lives out these truths in his day to day life. The result? Stability... inward nourishment...fruitfulness...strength and durability...and ultimate success.

Today, seek wise counsel as your first step.

Any given day as we watch the news, there is someone on trial for something. We have a law in the United States that every man and woman deserves a fair trial.

As a culture we are fascinated with trials, just turn on any television and you will be provided with numerous court shows of all kinds.

But this reminds me - when Jesus was arrested, He went through a half-dozen religious and state trials in just one night, without ANY legal representation.

As Jesus was shuttled from the Romans to the Sanhedrin and Caiaphas to Pilate, no one was there on His behalf to say, "I object." There was no legal dream team to make motions, or ask for a stay of execution.

The greatest leader history will ever know stood before one court after another and was accused of being what He was and is: GOD.

When you are accused, reflect on the humility and leadership of Jesus.

Today, no matter what anyone says, stay true to who you are.

The leaders God uses to the maximum are servant leaders.

Jesus was that IDEAL leader, in great part, because He was the IDEAL servant.

He humbled Himself. He who was rich became poor. He who was Lord of the Heavens and earth, arrived in flesh on this planet to a poor family, from a poor town that had a poor reputation. And in His adult life, He owned no property but the clothes he wore.

Jesus came to serve, not be served. He washed feet. He bore our sins. He died a sacrificial death.

God uses *servant leaders* to the maximum.

As you lead today, are you serving?

How to Respond Appropriately
to Challenges

As leaders, we must always respond appropriately to challenges.

The book of Joel in the Bible is fairly small, but it is full of impact. In the last chapter of the book, Joel pronounces judgment on the nations by using Israel. Joel predicts that if Israel will first respond in obedience, then they will be blessed and eventually bring hope to others.

Leaders sometimes are put in awkward places in their lives. They may not be places of disobedience, but nevertheless they can be awkward. When those awkward moments come, and a leader finds themself as either an instrument of justice, or a recipient of justice, that leader must be careful to interpret the context, see the future and make plans on how to appropriately respond.

Just remember, if things are awkward for you right now, God is at work in your life.

Today, ask Him how to navigate through the challenges.

Leaders Uphold God's Standards

Leaders are held to a high standard.

Sometimes God's people want to live just like the rest of the world and not be identified as different. And that leads to God's people not wanting to be held to the higher standard that God desires.

In the Old Testament book of Amos, God wanted Israel to be a light to the nations. They were to exemplify the life all people were to live. God's heavy judgment fell because He held His people accountable to lead the world to Himself.

Now God is still doing that today. When God's people are drawn to be just like everyone else, God expects the leaders of His peoplehere on this earth to stand up and rally the saints toward Him and His standards - that's just what Godly leaders are supposed to do!

Are you living up to God's higher standard?

Do you have "destination disease?"

If you think you have arrived (or someday, can arrive) by achieving a certain position, acquiring a certain degree, or earning a certain level of income, then you are in danger of finding yourself in either the *comfort zone* or the *coasting zone*.

What are you doing to safeguard yourself from standing still or sliding back? If you want to lead in the future, you need to learn for the future...and begin to do what you see in the future in the present.

The best leaders are always growing and learning, and moving forward. Leaders never see their lives as getting to a destination on earth, but as a journey to travel until God calls them to heaven.

What are you doing today to make sure you're planning and growing for the future?

Personal Growth Plan

Do you have a plan for personal growth?

Working hard and putting in long hours is admirable, but it doesn't insure personal growth. Neither does promotion. I salute someone who gets a deserved promotion, but getting a new title doesn't always translate into new growth.

What will you do today, this week, this month, this year to actively grow? What book will you read? What trip will you take? What interview will you conduct with someone you look up to? What CD or podcast will you listen to before the end of the month to help you on your growth journey? What conferences are you going to attend that will stretch you as a leader?

To grow spiritually, to grow as a follower of Christ–that's the goal.

But I have to ask you, what's the plan today?

All leaders should have a growth environment.

If you possess any kind of leadership role, you should create a growth environment in your role that prompts and encourages personal growth and development. You can make people who work for you or with you better if you're creating an environment that discusses and evaluates things that can improve the workplace.

There is a menu of items you could offer to co-workers; books and CDs, that simply improve the quality of life where you spend a good part of your day. So, next time you read a good book on leadership, why not go out and buy two or more for your colleagues? Ask them to read it, and then offer opinions and listen to what they have to say on what they learned. It's a great way to start a growth environment at the office!

How will you create a growth environment in your life?

Every leader faces tough times.

And it's the tough times when leaders distinguish themselves and show who they really are. Leading others can be difficult and can take great courage. It's not that way all the time. About 95% of the decisions a CEO makes could be made by a reasonably intelligent high school graduate.

What is often required is just common sense. But CEOs don't get paid for those decisions. They get paid for the other 5%. CEOs get paid for tough calls–the hard decisions that can affect the other 95% of the organization. Every change, crisis or challenge requires a tough call. And it's the tough call that separates leaders from everyone else.

If you are currently facing a difficult decision, maybe it's time to make the tough call.

FEB DAY 14

The Love Test

Part of the test that comes with being a leader is the love test.

This is the challenge to love people and care for others regardless of who they are or whether or not they can help you be successful.

There are times that leaders have to draw a line in the sand. But taking a stand for your convictions doesn't mean that you have to stop loving someone who just doesn't agree with you, or doesn't love you back.

Responding with love and grace to those who are hard to love and lack grace is a test every leader has to pass if they want to go to higher levels of influence.

Today, who can you show love to?

Leaders have to be willing to do the things others are unwilling to do.

From strong leaders in the Bible to strong leaders today, the best leaders have to be willing to put themselves on the line. One writer notes: "the most striking thing about highly effective leaders is how little they have in common. What one swears by, another warns against. But one trait stands out: effective leaders are willing to take a risk."

A friend of mine defines faith as "taking a risk for the glory of God." That's what great leaders do best—they live by faith and are willing to do things that others are unwilling to do.

Here's what I know...if you are going to take people forward, you can't always play it safe. Progress often, if not always, requires risk!

Today, be willing to take a risk in order to move forward.

FEB DAY 16

The Tests of Courage

What is the true test of courage?

Author and speaker Chuck Swindoll says: "Courage is not limited to the battlefield or the Indianapolis 500 or bravery by catching a thief in your house. The real tests of courage are much quieter. They are the inner tests, like remaining faithful when nobody's looking, like enduring pain when the room is empty, like standing alone when misunderstood."

Great words!

Doing the right thing isn't always easy, but it is always necessary if a leader wants to have integrity and be effective. Every battle we face may appear to others to be on the outside, but the greatest battles we fight are within. Building a life which leads to courageous and hard decisions in leadership begins with having a life which works on integrity, honesty and faithfulness.

Today, be courageous.

FEB DAY 17

The Hard Call

As leaders, at some point we all have to make the hard call.

If you haven't already had the chance to distinguish yourself by making tough calls for the sake of your people and the betterment of your organization, don't lose hope. Believe me, your opportunity is going to come. If you keep doing the right things, and more and more people follow you, you will gain more responsibility and the spotlight will come.

And when things are going great and your leadership has never been more trusted, get ready, because here it comes–the opportunity to make a hard call. And the more responsibility you get, the tougher the calls are to make. So, get ready, prepare yourself, in the not too distant future, you're going to get the opportunity to distinguish and prove yourself...you're going to get to make the hard call!

Today, take some time to consider what future decisions that you will need to make and also, reflect on the hard calls from your past. How have you grown from those experiences?

Do you have a Northstar?

Where are you getting the life principles that are required to make the hard calls of leadership? Do you have an ethical compass? Do you have around you the moral and ethical grid work that you need to make your hard call? Or, are you making hard calls in a vacuum?

For me, the best place to find the framework of life is the Bible. God's eternal word is a lamp and light for me. It clears the cobwebs in my head and convicts me of where I fail myself, my employees, and my God as a leader.

God's Word also gives me hope—that I can trust Him to lead me to make the hard call and sustain me when the consequences of the hard call are examined and critiqued.

Today, take some extra time to get in God's Word.

**Are You a Climber
or a Connector?**

Have you ever been at a party and met people who are "climbers?"

These are the folks that while they're talking to you they're also looking around the room to see who else is there. You know the person...they are more interested in climbing than they are in connecting.

What about you? Are you a climber or a connector? Climbers are always aware who is ahead of them and who is behind them. They are "rank" conscious.

Or, are you a connector? Connectors just get out of the way of climbers and focus on where people are–they just want to connect with people and build a relationship. If that relationship goes forward, great! If not, that's fine too.

Connectors value others more than they value themselves. Connectors think more about who is on the journey with them and how they can come alongside them!

Today, how can you be a better connector?

The Power to Choose

One of the greatest powers in life that God gives us is the power to choose.

Without question, choices are the most determining factor in how our lives turn out. John Wooden says, "There is a choice you have to make in everything you do. So keep in mind that in the end, the choice you make, makes you." There is no question that the choices we make dictate the lives that we lead.

Some people make their lives difficult by making wrong choices. Others move through life with greater ease because they've made some very good choices. Regardless of which road a person takes, here's the truth: We don't always get what we want, but we do always get what we choose.

Today, choose well–choose wisely–choose Biblically.

Are You Teachable ?

Abraham Lincoln was one of the most teachable presidents.

When he began his career, he was not a great leader. But he grew into his presidency.

He was always an avid listener, and as president, he opened the doors of the White House to anyone who wanted to express an opinion to him.

Over time, he received hundreds of letters each month offering advice.

Now while he may not have embraced every opinion offered, he learned what people were thinking, why they were thinking it and why they thought it was important.

All in all, those letters helped Lincoln learn the pulse of the American people and helped him craft his presidency.

Lincoln was teachable. Are you?

Nothing energizes a person the way passion does!

The things that bring the greatest personal reward are the fire lighters in a leader's life. Tim Redman said, "There are many things that will catch the eye, but there are only a few things that will catch my heart."

Take time to reassess your leadership and priorities. Are you spread out all over the place? Or are you focusing on the few things that bring the greatest reward? The greatest success comes only when you focus on what really matters.

Leaders never grow to the point where they no longer need to prioritize. It's something that good leaders keep doing all the time.

What are your priorities today? What is your number one priority? This is where your heart lies.

When it comes down to it, success is largely a matter of keeping the main thing the main thing.

William Gladstone put it this way: "He is a wise man who wasted no energy on pursuits for which he is not fit; and he is wiser still, who from among the things he can do well, chooses and resolutely follows the best."

Successful people don't allow the unimportant things in their lives to become important. Conversely, they don't allow the important things to become unimportant. They form a habit of spending their best resources on their best pursuits. Look at it this way, they ordered their activities so that they're always gravitating toward success.

Are your best resources spent on your best pursuits?

As leaders, we are blessed when we focus on the important things.

Every time Peter in the Bible focused on what was important, God blessed his actions. At Pentecost, Peter waited for God to prepare the hearts of the people before speaking to them and 3,000 people believed and were saved. Before the religious courts of the day, he refused to quit preaching because he knew that listening to God was more important than listening to men. And when the Grecian Jews complained about their limited food supply, Peter delegated the task to seven capable men so that he and other leaders could concentrate on their mission to preach the gospel.

Great leaders sift through many things that demand their time and can discern not only what needs to be done first, but also what doesn't need to be done at all.

Peter was passionate about everything, but he learned that there were just a few things that only he could do well.

How are you managing your time? Today, make sure you are delegating and focusing on the priorities that only you can do.

Learning How to Pack

Not too long ago, I went sailing with some friends for a few days in and around the Virgin Islands.

One of the big challenges was what to pack in our suitcases. Usually, even on a vacation, we tend to pack for at least a "dressy" night or two. But not on this trip! We were told to pack very light and very, very casual.

On the success journey, leaders have to learn how to pack. The less you take, the higher you can climb. But what you pack matters. On your success journey, who will you take with you?

What will YOU need to pack to become the success that God wants you to be?

Have you ever met anyone who just wasn't able to prioritize? Someone who gave more attention to the trivial instead of the important? I'd guess you would never define that kind of person as "successful." In all likelihood, that's a person who has never set and accomplished goals.

Goals matter. Goals help you determine what's first, second and third in life and responsibilities. Goals direct you and they measure you. Mark it down: successful people in any arena of life must have clear, attainable goals.

No one fulfills their purpose, reaches their potential or adds value to others without goals.

Today, take some time to write a list of attainable goals.

Here's a question for a leader: Do you believe enough in the people you lead, to invest extra time and energy into their personal growth and development?

Here's a challenge for a leader: Instead of enduring their shortcomings and failures, take them further than they could have ever traveled on their own—by being willing to invest in their lives.

It really is worth the effort. Jesus said when someone asks you to walk a mile with them, walk the second mile too. When you invest the "extra mile" in the lives of others, the return will be significant.

You see, the best leaders pour out their lives into others, like a drink offering. That's leading like Jesus.

Who can you invest in today?

Growing relationships take time and effort.

If you've ever tended a garden, you know the realities of soils and plants. First, plants don't grow overnight. They take time. Next, plants require a lot of attention, a lot of water, nutrients and even weeding. As well, plants grow in direct proportion to the amount of time you invest in them.

It's the same with relationships. Good leaders know relationships grow slowly and require attention. You must choose to put something in before you can expect to get something out. Some people come into our lives for a reason. Others, for a season. But the best leaders surround themselves with relationships that last for a lifetime.

What relationships are you tending to today? Who are your life-timers?

It's important as leaders to invest in people, even if they aren't investing in you.

Genesis tells the story of Joseph during some of his darkest hours. Joseph was a leader who kept investing in every relationship he encountered, regardless of how he was treated in return. Every success he achieved seemed to be followed by adversity, where his integrity and competence were challenged.

Whether he was sold into slavery, framed as an adulterer or forgotten in prison, Joseph would not be deterred from continuing to cultivate relationships in his life. Joseph had competence and character, but he also had a personality that valued people even when some of the people didn't value him.

Are you loving people in spite of how they treat you? Take time out of your day to show kindness to someone who may not necessarily deserve it.

How do you connect to someone 99% different than you?

People who are different and disagree often turn each other off. In fact, a relationship like that can become really hard work. How do you get along with a person who has little in common with you?

Life does not always allow us to be surrounded by the most pleasant of people. Therefore, leaders must find some way that they can connect with everyone. It's the 101% principle. Leaders must find the 1% they can agree on with someone and give it 100% of their attention.

So go ahead, leader. Give that 101% principle a try. Remember, the happiest people don't HAVE the best of everything; they just MAKE the best of everything.

Today, name one person in your life who you can use this principle to better connect with and begin applying!

Most leaders struggle with being patient.

They pray, "God, give me patience, and give it to me NOW." The fact that we are leaders means we are going somewhere; we have goals and dreams and we want to see the results. Waiting on others to understand and take the journey with us often feels long and difficult.

But remember leader, traveling alone may be quick, but we have no one with us to celebrate at the end of the journey. Traveling together allows leaders to share the joys of victory–but it almost always takes longer to get there and requires patience.

Today, who do you need to be more patient with?

The true test of relationships is not only how loyal we are when friends fail, but how thrilled we are when friends succeed.

This is a challenging issue to discuss, much less to face as leaders. But the scripture tells us to rejoice with those who rejoice!

It's not always easy to rejoice with the success of someone else. Jealousy can set in. We begin to feel envious as we compare their good fortune to ours. We experience pride and competition. While we pretend to rejoice in their success, secretly we can get angry that it was them, not us, who succeeded.

Secure leaders, secure people rejoice in the success of others. Insecure leaders, insecure people, DON'T. How about you?

Who can you rejoice with today?

Servant Leaders

Leaders have to be first and foremost, servants.

Eugene Habecker said, "The true leader serves...serves the people. Serves their best interests, and in so doing will not always be popular, may not always impress. But because true leaders are motivated by loving concern rather than a desire for personal glory, they're willing to pay the price."

What great words!

You've got to love your people more than your position. The early church knew that kind of servant leader in Barnabas. He took the initiative and whatever it took to raise morale, to raise up men and women, even raise money, Barnabas got the job done. He led others with the noble example of becoming a servant leader—of Jesus Christ.

Today, in what ways can you better serve those you lead?

The high road is the only road–when it comes to relationships.

It turns out that the high road is a road less traveled in our world today. But the Golden Rule reigns in the lives of people who take the high road.

High road leaders become instruments of grace, not guilt. High road leaders offer love over legalism. They offer the best to everyone, despite how they may have been treated.

High road leaders have as their model, the Lord Jesus. It was Jesus who took the ultimate high road by setting an example for us through service and through sacrifice on the cross.

High road leaders bring out the best in everyone.

Are you bringing out the best in those around you?

Taking the high road often means taking the harder road less traveled.

In Genesis, Abraham and Lot reach an impasse. Both had so much material stuff that a conflict arose among their employees. It turns out that there wasn't enough space for both of them to remain in the same territory. It would have been easy for Abraham to insist on getting his way. After all, he was the older one and the most influential.

But Abraham didn't demand his own way. He allowed Lot to choose which piece of land he wanted. Lot got first choice!

What an example of high road leadership. Abraham wasn't keeping score. He wasn't trying to get his own way. You see, he knew life was too short to live like that. And it's too short for us to live like that too. That's life on the high road.

How are you choosing to be a high road leader in your daily life?

Why do many relationships fail?

Some marriages start with passion and end in bitterness. Friendships start with hope and fizzle out. Ministries start with a promise and end in implosion. It's the same in business. Why?

Well, the reasons for such breakdowns are many, but the cause that outweighs them all is broken trust.

Remember this: Relationships are the currency of God's Kingdom. If we fail at relationships, we fail spiritually. Relationships matter—and they rise and fall on trust. We need friends that stick closer than a brother—friends we can trust.

Who are the friends you trust in your life?

MAR

A Virtuous Woman

"Who can find a virtuous woman?" Well, one of virtues' best role models could be found in Montreat, North Carolina. Her name was Ruth Graham.

Mrs. Graham personified the saying that "leadership is influence." She had no title, no public position, and rarely spoke to the press, but no one questions that this gentle yet determined woman was a leader–a woman of influence.

While Billy Graham traveled the world, she stayed home and raised five children. Her walk with God and her sense of humor enabled her to live a most remarkable life as the wife of the man who has told more people about Jesus than anyone else in human history.

Ruth Graham. Absent from the body. Present with the Lord!

The attitude you have today can have lasting impact on the leader you will become. What legacy of leadership will you leave behind?

**The Value of People
and Relationships**

Leaders must determine what's most important to them—and sadly many leaders ignore the high value of people and relationships.

They choose to focus on projects over people. And sometimes, sadly, they'll prioritize results at the expense of relationships.

The best leaders just don't do this. They recognize that people are their most appreciable asset, when people are loved and developed. Successful leaders don't allow the situation at any moment to become more important than the relationship.

Here's a question: When tough times come, what will be more important to you—the SITUATION or the PERSON?

The Bible teaches us that Joseph not only had a good mind, but a good heart—always taking the high road.

Now think about it: When his brothers realized Joseph was in charge of their fate, they were terrified—after all, they had left Joseph in a pit for dead! But Joseph, instead of retaliation, offers blessing. He puts his relationship with them ahead of the circumstances they deserved.

Joseph did what helped his family. He gave them food—and most importantly, he gave them forgiveness. He empowered instead of punishished. If you want to learn to be the kind of leader God uses, learn from Joseph.

Value relationships and be secure enough NOT to retaliate. The high road is the only road!

Make the high road of relationships your road for today.

Bob's the Problem!

Consider this: If Bob has problems with Paul, and Bob has problems with Elizabeth, and Bob has problems with John, and Bob has a problem with Linda... guess what?

BOB'S THE PROBLEM!

Sometimes when a person has issues with others–that person is the issue.

We all know people who seldom blame themselves for the problems they face. They always seem to look outward fixing the blame on someone else.

Consequently, problems just seem to follow these people around. The "Bobs" in life are problem carriers.

The lesson for today? Watch out for Bob!

The New Testament mentions a variety of men named "Herod." Every Herod in the Bible was a bad leader. They were all driven by their egos.

Herod the Great is the one who had the babies killed after Jesus was born.

Herod Antipas is the one who beheaded John the Baptist.

Herod Agrippa could not be persuaded about the Lordship of Christ.

Problems followed the Herods everywhere they went.

You could create a seminar on these guys about what <u>not</u> to do in leadership. Leaders who mistreat their citizens, act irrationally and are blinded by their egos are a concern.

Today, pray for the Herods of this world, their citizens and also for God to exercise His justice, in His time.

When preparing for battle, dig a foxhole big enough for a friend.

In the battles of life, foxholes take on different shapes and sizes. Our home, our work, our sports teams are just a few examples. It's in these foxholes that we develop a close relationship with others. When life gets tough, we need friends to stand with us.

Recent research says that tough times without friends is unhealthy. If you isolate yourself, you are twice as likely to die an early death… not to mention the possibility of emotional stress and depression.

So, if you're about to go into battle, grab a shovel and dig a foxhole big enough for two. You'll be glad you did.

To build trust as a leader, you must be honest about who you are. You must be authentic.

Emerson said, "The glory of friendship is not the outstretched hand, not the kindly smile, not the joy of companionship; but it is the spiritual inspiration that comes to one when you discover that someone else believes in you and is willing to trust you with a friendship."

What kind of person must you be in a relationship in order to be worthy of another person's trust? Well, it begins by trusting yourself.

If you are not honest with yourself, you will not be capable of being honest with others. Self deception is the enemy of relationships. If a person doesn't admit his shortcomings, he cannot improve them.

Be completely honest about who you are today. Then you can grow into the leader that others will want to follow!

Build Trust

If you are going to follow a leader for the long haul, you have to trust that leader.

Samson is a heartbreaking example of a leader who failed to build trust. Samson could have been one of Israel's greatest leaders, but when all was said and done, he turned out to be one of the worst.

If you look at Samson's life, you see a pattern of negative behavior that spelled trouble–in his relationship with God and others. And it all came back to credibility...trust!

Leaders who find the ground of trustworthiness eroding beneath their feet, usually fail to deal with their character weaknesses and are amazingly deceptive.

Are there any signs of trouble like this in your life?

A leader must always have a firm grasp on the right perspective.

What if you had the opportunity of a lifetime to fulfill your dreams? What if only one person stood between you and your goal? It is very easy to let a situation become so important to us that we fail to show sensitivity to our friends, family, even co-workers. Sometimes we win an argument but lose a friendship!

Anytime a person puts the situation ahead of a relationship, it happens for one reason - loss of perspective.

To keep your perspective and prevent the situation and relationship from deteriorating, ask yourself: Am I putting projects and deadlines in front of people?

Your mission is the foundation of your priorities.

In the Book of Acts, when Peter understood that his mission was to spread Christianity, that became the foundation of all his other decisions. From that point on everything Peter did supported the direction that he was going.

And yet he didn't always have total vision beginning on day one.

Now, maybe you are similar to the way Peter was at first—full of passion but lacking direction. The good news is that you already have half of the equation. The bad news is that if you don't know where you're going, you'll end up spinning your wheels. Or worse, you'll spend years going in the wrong direction.

When you're confident of where you should be headed, your priorities become clearer and your actions take on significant meaning.

Do you know what direction you are going in?

Strong leaders are always the first to recognize when a course of action needs to be taken, and they quickly consider how to go about it.

In the Book of Acts, Peter knew that if the Grecian Jews' request wasn't met, the church could lose momentum. Rather than trying to meet the needs all by himself, which a lot of leaders attempt, Peter determined that it wasn't his top priority and figured out another way.

As a leader how do you react when your people bring a genuine need before you? Do you stop what you're doing and immediately take care of it? Do you nod your head as if you're interested, then push it aside and forget about it?

Or like Peter, step back, take a look at the big picture and determine what action is appropriate according to your leadership priorities?

Today, take time to review the problems that are presented to you. Step back, assess and respond, deciding what actually needs to be addressed. Be a big picture leader!

When to Delegate

Leaders know when to delegate.

Peter and the disciples set up their team in the early church for success. They not only made sure that the seven men selected were well suited to meet the needs at hand, but also presented them to the people as worthy leaders. In doing so, they built trust and confidence in the men to succeed.

Many leaders are so driven that they hurriedly delegate the task just to be able to check it off their "to do" list. They falsely perceive delegation as a way of decreasing distractions, instead of increasing effectiveness.

Great leaders understand that their effectiveness is a function of their people's success, and they make it a priority to help them succeed.

How are you delegating your tasks in a way that is promoting success?

Missionary Amy Carmichael wisely noted, "We will have all eternity to celebrate the victories, but only a few hours before sunset to win them."

Without the limitation of time, there might be no need to prioritize. But time limits you and forces you to make choices. The more time you spend on the wrong things, the less time you have to invest in what is <u>right</u>.

When you learn to spend your time wisely on the things that bring your organization the most success, you often wind up with - get this - time to spare.

In short, being successful is not about how <u>hard</u> you work, it's about how <u>smart</u> you work.

Today, take time to prioritize your day so that you can make the right choices no matter the time limitation.

As leaders with limited time, we must learn to work smart.

As pointed out yesterday, when you learn to spend your time wisely you often end up with time to spare. Being successful is not about how <u>hard</u> you work; it's about how <u>smart</u> you work.

There's a story I often tell at conferences about a man who was told that if he worked the very hardest job he would become successful and rich. The hardest job he could do was digging holes, so he began digging <u>huge</u> holes in his backyard, each one bigger than the other.

But in the end, he didn't get rich. He got a backache.

You see, he spent a lot of time working hard, but worked with no purpose, and he sure didn't work smart.

What large pointless holes are you digging in your life right now? Prioritize your time by being smart about your work.

What is the true nature of leadership?

Many people today want to climb up the corporate ladder because they believe that freedom and power are the prizes waiting for them at the top. What they don't realize is that the true nature of leadership is <u>sacrifice</u>.

Leaders who want to succeed have to do more that take an occasional cut in pay. They have to give up their rights and, often times, their privileges. That's true of any leader, regardless of profession.

Talk to any leader and you'll find that he or she has made repeated sacrifices. And usually the higher the leader has climbed, the greater the sacrifices that leader has made. Effective leaders sacrifice much that is good in order to dedicate themselves to that which is best.

What are you sacrificing in the pursuit of God's greatness?

MAR DAY 24

**Sacrifice to Become
a Great Leader**

If you doubt that sacrifice can be separated from leadership, just read the Word of God.

Time after time leaders had to make sacrifices to be the leaders that God created them to be. Often, the greater the calling, the greater the sacrifice.

Noah was one of the first people in the Bible to make great sacrifices to become a leader. He started over from scratch after surrendering all, even his family's understanding, to obey God. Abraham did the same and so did Joseph.

In effect, anyone greatly used by God understands the importance of sacrifice. Leadership always has a cost. To be a leader you many not be asked to leave your country or give up all your possessions, but you can be sure of this, leading always has a price.

Today, reflect on the price of leadership in your own life. Are you willing to give up in order to become the leader God is calling you to be?

A leader must pursue the heart of God to experience victory.

Have you ever thought about what separates the leaders who achieve victory from those who suffer defeat? What does it take to be a winner? It's hard to put a finger on one quality that separates a winner from a loser, but let me give it a shot.

Great leaders share an inability to accept defeat. The alternative to winning seems totally unacceptable to them, so they figure out what they must do to achieve victory, to go after it with great gusto.

In the Word of God, King Josiah was a man who sought God, experienced personal breakthroughs, and who allowed for victory. It says that Josiah was right in the sight of the Lord. He walked in the ways of his father, David.

When you, as a leader, pursue the heart of God, you have taken the first step toward a life of winning, a life of victory.

MAR

DAY 26

Let God Work in Your Life

To be a winner, you must allow God to work in your life.

Most people secretly believe that winners achieve what they do because they have it easier than everyone else. They are lucky. They have more talent. They are born into the right family. In other words, their circumstances are better than ours. That's just not true most of the time!

People who succeed often do so because they are able to overcome terrible odds and miserable circumstances. If a leader faces a deck stacked against him or her, that leader has to start overcoming obstacles in his or her life.

In the Bible, King Josiah faced major obstacles. He was only eight years old when be became King. He came from a legacy of leaders during some of Israel's worst times. He didn't have a positive role model around him. And yet he ruled a nation with great leadership.

No matter the obstacles you may face, let today be the day that you allow God to work in your life.

I think just about everybody loves to win, but what about the battle within?

There's nothing like the celebration that follows the big win. Most people like receiving the winner's prize. It's a mark of achievement. But the danger of focusing on the prize is that we may come to a point when victory is something that occurs outside us. Winning is really an inside job.

The team that achieves victory is one comprised of individuals who first win their internal battles. The first person on any team who must face and win these internal battles is the leader.

In God's Word, King Josiah is a great example of someone who dealt with his inner issues. Because he got victory over them, he brought victory to his team and to his nation.

Here's a question: Are you taking responsibility for your victories?

Have you ever experienced being on a roll?

Some people call it being in the zone. Everything goes right, every customer says yes and no matter how hard you try not to make it work, it works for you.

If you have experienced that kind of thing as a leader, you know what its like. It's called momentum. When it comes to achievement in an organization, momentum is a leader's very best friend.

In God's Word, King Saul lacked momentum in his life. In contrast, at the same time, young David was creating momentum in his life. If you study the lives of both men, you grow to understand why Saul lacked momentum and why David was gaining it. King Saul was focusing on King Saul. And David was focusing on God.

Hey leader, where is your focus today? The answer may reflect how you're doing on the scale of momentum.

If you as a leader could ask for and receive any gift, what would you choose?

Would you pick a few quality leaders to have on your team? Or would you prefer immense material resources? How about better facilities?

In the Bible Solomon picked wisdom, but he was able to choose that because of the luxury of the momentum his father David had already given him as a legacy. That wisdom enabled him to have all the other things he needed, including greater momentum.

The time of transition from one leader to another is the most critical time in continuing momentum. When Solomon took over in David's role, he already started with what David had provided.

He kept the peace and he humbly asked for wisdom as a leader.

If you could ask for any gift, what would it be? There's nothing quite like wisdom!

Success always comes with a price.

That's a lesson every one should learn in childhood. We can pay now and play later or we can play now and pay later. Either way, we are going to have to pay.

Creating a climate for potential leaders requires a leader that is willing to pay the price. It all begins with personal growth. If an organization is going to grow, be it a church, a business or any kind of entity, a leader will dictate the growth of the organization by his or her own personal growth.

Leaders must examine themselves, ask hard questions of themselves, and then determine to do the right thing regardless of atmosphere or mood. The most successful leaders recognize that personal growth and development of leadership skills are lifetime pursuits.

Are you willing to pay the price to be a perpetual leader?

One of the mistakes rookie leaders often make is that they try to lead everyone the exact same way. If we are honest, everyone does not respond to the same kind of leadership.

One person may respond to being challenged, while another may respond to being nurtured. One will need the game plan drawn up for them, while another is motivated to draw up the game plan for themselves. One will require constant follow-up, while another will require lots of breathing room.

If you and I want to be effective leaders, we have to be willing to adjust our leadership styles to where our people are, not necessarily expecting them to adapt to us.

In what ways will you strive to be a more effective leader?

Think about two or three areas of life that are most important to you.

Don't you think it might be a good use of your time to sit down and match these areas along with some disciplines that you need to develop to keep growing and improving in these areas?

To develop a plan to make daily or weekly disciplines that will enhance your values and belief systems is one of the most profitable uses of time one can imagine.

"The best time to plant a tree is 25 years ago" a sign says, "The second best time is today." Plant the tree of self-discipline in your life today.

Today, take time to write the benefits to practicing the disciplines you list. Put those benefits in a place where you can see them every single day.

No Substitute for Enthusiasm!

There is no substitute for enthusiasm!

When the members of the team are enthusiastic, the whole team becomes highly energized. And that energy produces power. Industrialist Charles Schwab observed, "People can succeed at almost anything for which they have enthusiasm."

How are you doing when it comes to enthusiasm related to your faith in Jesus Christ? As a leader who knows Christ, is your enthusiasm the freshest and most optimistic that it's ever been?

If you want to be enthusiastic in life, ask the Lord in a very fresh way to immerse your mind and emotions in things that honor Him.

Growth Determines Who You Are

Leaders face the danger of contentment when they embrace the status quo.

After all, if a leader already possesses influence and has achieved a level of respect, why should they keep growing?

Well, try these answers on for size. Your growth determines who you are. Who you are determines who you attract. Who you attract determines the success of your organization.

If you want to grow your organization, you have to remain teachable. The Bible tells us that we reap what we sow. So, what kind of crop are you reaping in your life?

When was the last time you did something for the very first time?

On the road to Calvary, Jesus Christ experienced loneliness like no other leader in human history.

In the Garden of Gethsemane the *God-Man* settled the issue of His crucifixion in His unique relationship with His Heavenly Father.

From Gethsemane, all the way to Calvary, EACH step He took exemplified sacrifice to perfection.

The next time you're asked by God to sacrifice for the good of your family, your colleagues or for some Kingdom purpose, draw strength and courage from the Savior, whose ultimate sacrifice makes our sacrifices look small by comparison.

Hanging between two thieves on Calvary's Cross and in front of hundreds of onlookers, Jesus was still leading... still influencing.

In near agony and pain, sacrificing for the sins of a lost world, Jesus was influencing those on his left and right, and those in front of the cross and behind it.

The world may not understand it, but when a leader sacrifices for others, their leadership LEAPS to new levels of influence.

Sacrifice on the cross made a difference for eternity. Sacrifice in your marriage, or for your team members or your congregation. You can make a major difference today.

Every Easter, followers of Christ are publicly reminded of the great and eternal work of the Savior on the cross and through the resurrection.

A Christian's public identification with Easter IS important—especially as it seems our world is increasingly secular in thought and public policy.

However, every Easter should prompt Christ followers to take a fresh look at who Jesus is, and continues to be in our internal lives. May the words of our great and sacrificing leader never leave our vocabulary! He is the way, the truth and the life—and no one, he said, could have a relationship with God the Father, but through Him, Jesus Christ.

Again this Easter, give praise and worship to our great and wonderful leader, Jesus Christ.

Every once in a while, I'll read an article or watch a television interview where some skeptic seems to relish in attempting to discount the life and leadership of Jesus Christ.

They'll be so bold even as to mock the meaning of His death–and with even more mockery, diminish that His resurrection was even a remote possibility.

I am reminded at times like Easter, that in an increasingly hostile world toward the things of the God-Man, we Christ-followers always need to be ready to give an account of the hope that's within us. The hope is all tied up in a "who"–not just a "what."

Jesus is our hope. He is our leader. Easter is a great reminder that it's a good idea to not only know the "who" but the "why."

When Jesus was on the cross–taking upon Himself our sin and shame, love took on a meaning that continues to be incomparable by act or definition.

Think of it: Jesus Christ died for my sin. If you belong to Him, He died for your sin too. Though our sins would be red like scarlet, thanks to what Jesus did on the cross, those same sins would be erased, whited out - just like fresh, fallen snow.

Jesus Christ is the greatest leader the world, universe, the galaxies–and galaxies beyond will ever know. His thirty-plus years on earth, His hours on the cross, His days in the tomb, His eternal existence following His resurrection, serve as solid reminders that our great Leader has conquered sin and the grave!

Good Friday for the skeptic is just another Friday. For Christ-followers, it's a day which historically, and more importantly, spiritually, vividly brings to the reminiscent mind, Jesus being nailed to a cross and dying for the sins of human kind.

In the 1700s, Charles Wesley wrote about the death of Jesus this way: "AMAZING LOVE, HOW CAN IT BE, THAT THOU MY GOD WOULD DIE FOR ME?"

Hey, I know you're busy—just like me. But wouldn't it be just the best of ideas to pause for awhile this week and just get quiet, and thank God for His amazing gift of love to us—who died for our sins...

His son, Jesus Christ.

Jesus Christ is the greatest leader the world has known or ever will know.

Line up every positive and affirming leadership characteristic you can name, and there you will find Jesus being defined– defined as the perfect 10, and beyond.

At Easter we are graphically reminded that our Perfect Savior took upon Himself non-perfection on the cross; that is, He took upon Himself all our sin.

In a world where leaders are often defined by cynics who say 'it's all about the leaders,' Jesus, on the cross, inverts that model and demonstrates, 'it's all about my followers.'

Pause this Easter Weekend and give thanks, my friend. There is a Savior, risen, living and coming again. He is the greatest leader the world will ever know.

Motion picture director James Cameron has hit an iceberg bigger than Titanic did with his recent claims that he has proof now that Jesus died 2000 years ago...and stayed dead.

Christians have heard all of this before. There was the Passover Plot in the 70's. Then, there was the Last Temptation of Christ in the 80's. More recently, there was the DaVinci Code.

All were efforts to discredit the "God" part of the God-Man.

Again this Easter, Christian leaders must boldly and without apology remind people of the importance that Jesus not only died for our sins, but rose from the dead...and never died again!

Christians have debated the subject of leadership for years. Is it Biblical to lead? Aren't we called to be *followers* instead of leaders?

When you study the Bible, you discover that leadership is God's idea. God is not only the ultimate leader, but He's called people like you and me to lead as well.

God gave us the responsibility and authority to reign over the earth. And God gave us the ability to do just that!

Based on your personality and gifts, YOU have the ability to lead in some area of life in this world. And you can begin by leading yourself.

Salt and Light

Being salt and light directly implies a LEADERSHIP role of setting an example... being a person of influence.

Salt influences the flavor of our food. Light influences the paths that we take and the things we see.

You see, being salt and light is being a person of influence...and a person of influence leads others!

Paul said, "Knowing the fear of God, we PERSUADE (or influence) men."

Jesus calls you and me to add flavor and to shine, to influence.

And that's what leadership is...influence.

Leadership is Influence

J. Oswald Sanders said it first: Leadership is influence. Nothing more, nothing less.

Leadership is about influencing others toward a worthwhile cause.

Leadership is NOT dependent on just titles or positions. It is dependent on someone catching a vision from God and mobilizing others to join them in its fulfillment!

Today, like never before, the world cries out for Godly, effective leaders. When we obey Jesus' teachings to be salt and light, we become people of influence—in front of our families, the local school board, the media, even the next door neighbor.

Leadership is influence. Nothing more... nothing less!

There are times when a leader has to make a hard decision.

Sometimes as leaders, a burden takes us late into the night, while our colleagues are sound asleep—and that burden takes us to our knees.

You may feel like that right now.

You feel alone. But in reality, you're not. Jesus Christ, the greatest of all leaders, understands. He faced the hardest decisions. He faced those decisions, humanly speaking, while all alone.

Know that today, you're NOT alone. Cast your leadership cares on Him and discover that His broad shoulders can handle them.

Passion, passion, passion!!!

When you display passion to those around you about a cause that is worthwhile, the passion spreads!

Passion doesn't require money. Money's great...but there are a lot of wealthy folks who wouldn't recognize passion if it gave them a kiss on the cheek.

Passionate people look beyond themselves to concentrate on the needs of others. They care for the homeless, build houses for the poor and visit those in prison. They preach Christ crucified and teach about great faith in God.

Passion is in great need today. And the great news is you don't need money to obtain it.

Today, reawaken your passion!

Got Heart?

Last year my doctor sent me to get a heart scan. In about 10 minutes this elaborate machine took pictures of my heart from just about every angle.

Every few days or so, leaders need to scan their hearts—not the muscle in the body, but the motive in the center of their being. Jesus said that out of the heart come the issues of life. In a day when good leadership is greatly needed, pure leadership is needed even more.

"Place your delight in the Lord and He will give you the desires of your heart." Psalm 36:4

Be a leader with the right motives, clean hands, and a pure heart!

A big part of being a leader is knowing your purpose in life...knowing WHY on earth God put you here.

Now there is a reason you're here, but do you know what that reason is?

You'll NEVER know fulfillment until you discover your purpose. And when you discover that, it will help you to decide to do the BEST things in life, not just the good things in life.

So ask God today...why am I here? What is it that you have called me to do? Think it through. Be quiet and listen to God. Then start jotting down what you're thinking.

Let God's thoughts become your thoughts.

Well, it's convicting, but necessary for a leader...asking *tough questions of ourselves!*

I don't like them, but here we go:

- Do I have sinful hindrances in my life?
- Are there moral ethical shortfalls in my leadership?
- How's my self discipline?
- Am I insecure, jealous?
- Do I have a critical spirit?

The leader God uses is constantly in need of answering tough questions about character and motive. No leader is perfect, but Jesus. But the questions we need to answer keep us focused on HIM and our need for Him every moment of our leadership journey.

You see, the leader God uses removes hindrances from his or her life.

Do you ever question the truth of the Scriptures?

A few years ago in New York City, a copy of a Shakespeare play sold at an auction for more than a million dollars. We have no originals of Shakespeare's plays, but the copies are celebrated as the real thing.

The Bible was copied more meticulously than any other document of literature in history. And leaders are wise when they seek the Scriptures for comfort and answers.

John C. Maxwell says, "Everything I know about leadership I learned from the Bible." The Bible has served John Maxwell's leadership needs over the years and it will serve your leadership needs too.

And that's more than a million dollars of good advice!

My attitude is contagious.

Several things are not contagious. Talent is not contagious, neither is experience. A willingness to practice is not contagious. But attitude, be it positive or negative, is contagious.

During the first half of the twentieth century, no one had run a mile in under 4 minutes in competition. But in 1954, Roger Banister did. Two months later, an Australian runner did too. Then dozens and hundreds more followed. It became contagious.

What happened? The attitude of the runners changed. They believed they could raise their running to a whole new level.

You see, people catch attitudes like they catch a common cold - by getting up close.

What kind of attitude are you spreading?

Keep It Simple

Good leaders value good communication; and they know good communicators keep the message simple.

Jesus shared most of His message through stories. In fact, in Matthew 17, He shared 7 different stories. Jesus used the power of simple, familiar narratives.

Someone said, "The educator makes the simple complex, but the communicator makes the complex simple."

When you think about what Jesus did, He gave the people a point for their heads, and He painted a picture for their hearts.

The success of your leadership, your marriage, your relationship with others depends a lot on your ability to communicate. A lot of your leadership rides on your ability to connect with people.

A public speaker usually puts the message before the people. But a communicator understands the value of putting the people before the message.

When Jesus spoke He saw the people and He perceived their needs. It's difficult to effectively communicate with an audience without caring about that audience. Jesus tied His communication to His character.

To be more like Jesus in our communication, we have to be more people-oriented than lesson-oriented. Jesus shows us that if you focus on people, the lesson will last longer.

Today, be a leader like Jesus–focus on people.

Are you passionate about the ideas you are communicating?

Someone said, "There are no boring subjects, only boring speakers." Well, that may be true. However, every effective communicator I've ever heard was passionate about their subject. And more times than not, their subject matter came from some kind of inner conviction.

Jesus did not communicate out of routine or obligation. He spoke from the convictions of His heart.

The next time you speak on a subject, own it. Know the subject well. Present it in a manner that says, "Hey, I'm passionate about this!"

Let the world know today, that not only are the words coming from your mouth; they're coming from your heart.

The Bible is clear that leaders are to select and train people for a life of ministry.

Jesus selected and trained twelve. Paul found young men like Titus and Timothy. A "Timothy" is someone who is following you in his or her leadership, but is eager to grow as a leader as well.

Every leader ought to have apprentices who learn as they serve alongside the leader. In fact, when they learn, they are also called to pass on what they receive.

A leader's ministry may add to the Kingdom. But when they train a disciple, that leader multiplies for the Kingdom.

Do you have any "Timothy's" in your life that you are discipling for God's glory?

If you see a need around you, do something about it!

Perceiving a need in your community could become a catalyst of your leadership journey. Moses saw the need of liberating his people from slavery. Joseph saw the need to keep his constituency from starving and Nehemiah saw the need to rebuild the walls of a defenseless city.

What are the needs where you live? Mentoring? Caring for the elderly? A reading program? Reaching out to expectant moms?

Leaders perceive a need and then they act on it...in response to the need.

What would happen, if today, you took one step toward meeting a need in your community? What impact would it have? What difference would it make?

Automatic Growth

Growth is not automatic.

There is a misconception out there that personal growth and development is automatic. The fact is that if we don't take personal responsibility for our growth,it just won't happen.

If you believe growth simply comes with age,you are mistaken. You have to work at it. It's an illusion to believe that waiting around for something to happen to you, or watching just another television show is going to make you better.

Personal growth and development begins when *you* decide that *you* want to grow. One Pulitzer prize winning composer said it this way, "Hell begins on that day when God grants us a clear vision of all that we might have achieved, of all the gifts that we wasted, and all that we might have done and did not do."

There's been a tribe in Central Asia which cursed an enemy not by using force or evil spirits, but by simply saying, 'May you simply stay in one place, forever.'

Thatto me seemslike the ultimate curse for someone who doesn't understand the need forpersonal growth and development. There's nothing worse than getting stuck in one place, getting stuck in life and not having a clue about how to get out.

If you don't try to improve your life every single day, you're going to have the same results of going absolutely nowhere. You'll be stuck in the same place, doing the same thing, hoping the same hopes, and with every day that passes never gaining new ground, or winning new victories.

How are you stuck? Don't stay in one place forever. Do something!

A St. Louis doctor met a high school kid who had lost his hand at the wrist. When the doctor started to inquire about the handicap the teenager replied, "I don't have a handicap sir, I just don't have a right hand."

Life's greatest handicap is a person who isn't realizing their potential. People who have no dreams to fulfill are emotionally paralyzed, immobile and have a very difficult time functioning in society.

If you are focusing more on what you <u>don't</u> have instead of what you <u>do</u> have, take a deep breath and remind yourself that God has designed you to maximize your potential in spite of some of life's greatest obstacles.

Have you ever set growth goals?

No, I'm not talking about weight gain or making yourself taller. I'm talking about setting a personal growth plan for your lifeand your leadership. Planning your growthwill increase your understanding about who youare, and benefit you on just about every levelin life.

While you are growing in grace and knowledge of the Lord Jesus, you can grow like Jesus grew in His humanity. He grew in wisdom and in favor with God and with people. Personal growthgoals, things like working on your attitude, communication skills, time management, parenting skillscan all make your life grow in grace and knowledge.

Take a moment to assess your growth goals and begin today!

There are certain species of fish that will grow according to the size of their environment. In a tiny aquarium, they will remain tiny through adulthood. But, put them out to sea and they will grow to their naturally intended size.

It is the same with you and me. Put us in a dysfunctional, negative, controlling environment and we find ourselves staying small and trapped. But put us in an environment that encourages growth, hope and optimism, watch out, we will expand and start to reach our potential.

What kind of environment are you in? Who are you hanging around? What kind of atmosphere are you creating for your children?

Make up your mind today, to put yourself in a growth environment and watch what happens.

Knowledge is useless if it's not applied.

Have you ever known someone who was so smart, and knew a lot of "stuff" but just didn't have the skill to help someone else with all they knew?

John Maxwell puts it this way, "Individuals like that are similar to encyclopedias: they are filled with information but useless when unused."

Life change really is the measure of whether information makes a difference. As you run from one conference to the next, listen to one program after another and read books and this and that, what are you doing with this information?

The best leaders learn, then they apply, and then it flows from them to others.

Good leaders embrace good values.

Years ago, James Dobson spoke at a university commencement about the mid-life crisis phenomenon that seems to occur between the ages of 35 to 50. He said, "I believe it is more a phenomenon of wrong values than it is the age group of which it occurs. All of the sudden you realize the ladder you've been climbing is leaning against the wrong wall."

Like never before, leaders, moms, dads, bosses, public leaders and business people need to clarify and embrace good values.

You don't want a mid-life crisis. Chase after God's values today so that you don't find yourself living the first half of your life climbing that ladder only to discover it's leaning against a building that doesn't reflect your values at all.

Today, spend some time thinking about the values you want your life to reflect.

Having good values is like having a Northstar in your life.

When things get crazy and life throws all kinds of changes at you, both good and bad, your values are what keep you on track. They keep you focused, grounded and moving in the right direction.

Life changes, values don't. Methods change, values don't. You change and grow, but values don't.

You see, there are just a few good values to embrace, and God gives them to us in His Word.

What are your core values? Have you ever written them down?

If you have, can you put your hands on them to review them? In a crazy, messed up sin-stained world, you need a Northstar and your values can help you stay the course.

When it comes to money and things, how are you defined? Are you known as generous, or selfish?

If you aren't clear as to how you are seen by others on this issue, why not ask your spouse or best friend to tell you the truth.

I find it very sad and de-motivating to be around people who have a scarcity mentality. They don't want to give, they want to keep. They don't want to share, they want to stock up. They don't live by faith, they live in fear.

You say, 'well, I'm not rich.' Well here's a newsflash: a person's income level and will to give have nothing to do with one another. Some of the most generous people I know on this planet have very little material possessions.

Don't wait for your income to change; change your heart today.

Giving Your Best

Recently, John Maxwell and John Hull were in Bolivia together. The people there were thrilled to have Dr. Maxwell come and minister.

As they approached an indoor arena where John Maxwell was about to speak, we heard a band playing. In honor of John Maxwell, about a dozen Bolivians were playing a song about hospitality and honor.

John Hull leaned over to Maxwell and said, "Hey boss, they're giving you their very best. In this poor country they're wearing their best clothes, playing their best instruments and playing their best song to express how much they appreciate you being here."

By now, he had big tears in his eyes.

Generous people don't need to have a lot of material possessions to express their generosity.

If you're waiting to get rich before you become generous, you're fooling yourself. Start where you are, and start giving.

As leaders, we must first learn to lead ourselves.

All of us have some good habits, and some bad ones too. A habit is anything you and I do without thinking about it. Habits have power that can kill a dream, or create a more healthy body. Bad habits can cause you to go through the motions. Good habits cause you to think about the possibilities of what might be.

Good leaders, before they can ever effectively lead others, first lead themselves. Good leaders establish healthy habits and routines and deliberately work on trying to eliminate the negative habits that can lead to distraction or destruction.

Is there a habit you need to *kick*? Or is there a habit you need to *kickoff*? The best leaders know the difference between the two, and act accordingly.

Dreams! One leadership authority said that "dreams are like soap bubbles floating close to jagged rocks on a windy day." His point: Dreams can be fragile.

Now you may not be short on dreams, but you may be running a bit of a deficit in protecting and nurturing those dreams. Dreams need time to grow and develop. The best leaders dream great dreams, but they give those dreams time to get planted into some good soil and take root.

There's something about human nature that wants to pour water on your dreams. Like jagged rocks and high winds, they want to pop your bubbles of hope. But don't let them.

Keep dreaming...and start protecting and nurturing those dreams. Perhaps one day, those dreams will come true!

When you share your dreams with family or friends, what kind of reaction do you get?

Do you get, "That's great!" Or, do you get, "Well, that's nice...now pass me the potato salad." Some people just don't know how to respond positively to a dreamer like you. But don't let that, or them, keep you from dreaming great dreams!

The next time you are hesitant to share your dream with someone because you're fearful of their possible negative reaction, take a deep breath of courage and share the dream anyway. It will be good practice for you–because this won't be the last time someone won't be too thrilled about your dream.

Undeveloped dreams can create undeveloped talent, undeveloped resources, and undeveloped relationships. Keep dreaming, my leader-friend. There's so much to be gained.

Not everyone is going to be thrilled when your dreams come true.

In fact, some will be like a firefighter; they will put out your fiery dream so fast–they'll criticize and you can't change their minds.

Then, there will be fire-starters. They will be so moved by your dream that they will come alongside you and do whatever they can to fan the flames of success.

Good leaders are rarely surprised by which people will be firefighters or fire-starters. But here's the deal for you...don't let anyone take your focus off the dream that God has given you. If God birthed the dream in your heart, God will bring that dream to a reality, sooner or later.

No matter how long it takes, don't lose YOUR fire!

DAY 11

Tribute to Jerry Falwell

Jerry Falwell was a man with great influence.

He influenced hundreds of thousands of people through founding Liberty University. He influenced a local congregation, Thomas Road Baptist Church, starting it in the 1950's and growing it from a handful of people to 24,000 people today.

He was a controversial person and many did not always agree with Jerry, including me. But he still had great influence. He worked very, very hard to try to make this world better for the glory of God.

Today, we honor Jerry Falwell and other leaders like him who influence the Kingdom and strive to make our nation and world a better place.

When Jerry Falwell died, what crossed your mind when you heard the news?

The first thing that crossed my mind is I could still remember seeing Jerry Falwell standing on Liberty Mountain casting vision about building a great university for the glory of God in the United States. And with the power of God upon him, Jerry Falwell built that university.

Today his legacy lives on, not only through Liberty, but also through the Thomas Road Baptist Church. Jerry Falwell was a person of passion and was a person of influence. Today make a difference in your schools, in your church, in your community for the glory of God, and do it with passion.

One thing that Jerry Falwell knew in his life was that today matters.

I knew Jerry Falwell for decades and he was one of the hardest working people I ever saw or witnessed. He worked from sunup to sundown, midnight and beyond. For Jerry Falwell, today mattered. His eternal home now is in heaven. He's resting, but for us here there's still much to do.

Yesterday is history, tomorrow might not come, so do what you can today. Live your daily agenda in a manner that honors God, that honors your family and that makes a difference in all those around you.

If you're driving your car today, you know all about high gas prices first-hand. But, regardless of the price, you still know that you have to put fuel in your car's tank. Leaders understand, as well, that those they lead need fuel in their tanks too.

The people you lead are fueled by good resources like books, CDs and DVDs on personal growth and development. When you get the next opportunity, head to the bookstore or go on-line and purchase some resources that you can get into the hands of the people on your team.

They'll be grateful and your team will grow to another level. The next time you fill your car with gas, remember the need to fill up your colleagues with good resources!

A few years ago, Mike Wallace of 60 Minutes fame interviewed one of the Sherpa guides from Nepal who helps climbers reach the top of Mt. Everest. Wallace asked, "Why do you do it?"

"To help others do something they can't do on their own" was his answer.

Wallace said, "But there are so many dangers. Why do you insist on taking people to the top of the mountain?"

The guide smiled and said, "It's obvious that you've never been to the top."

If you're going to the top of any endeavor, it's going to take major league commitment. The road in front of you isn't traveled by many. Along the way, you will meet some who will help you and others who will hurt you. Those who will discourage or hurt you have never been to the top.

But the top of the mountain is where you want to go. It's worth every tiring step. It's worth the commitment.

Dreams are wonderful things for leaders to ponder. But dreams must be coupled with a positive attitude. You see, if you have one without the other, things get messed up real fast.

A dream without a positive attitude produces a DAYDREAMER.

A positive attitude without a dream produces a pleasant person who cannot progress in life.

A dream together with a positive attitude produces a person with unlimited possibilities and potential.

So, keep dreaming. But dream with an attitude that says, "With God's help, it can be done!"

Leaders must keep making progress.

When Spanish cellist Pablo Casals was in the final years of his life, a young reporter asked him, "Mr. Casals, you are ninety-five years old and the greatest cellist who ever lived. Why do you still practice six hours a day?"

Casals answered: "BECAUSE I THINK I'M MAKING PROGRESS." Now that's an example of an individual who is dedicated to personal growth and development.

People like Pablo Casals, Tiger Woods or Billy Graham kept and keep growing because no matter what success God gave them they were always looking at ways to improve their craft.

What about you? Are you growing? What are you reading? What are you watching? Who are you hanging around? Are you getting better? Are you, like, Casals, making progress?

Knowing What Counts

When I was a kid in the mid-sixties, no team dominated college basketball like John Wooden's UCLA Bruins. Wooden, now in his 90's has lived his life constantly growing and reaching personal bests. He was famous for saying: "It's what you learn AFTER you know it that counts."

Coach Wooden recognized that the greatest obstacle to growth isn't ignorance, but KNOWLEDGE. The more you learn, the more puffed up you can get and the more you can think that you know it all. And that leads to being a KNOW IT ALL. And that leads, quite frankly to loneliness and limitations.

When you remain teachable, your potential is just about absent of borders. It's what you learn AFTER you know it all that really counts.

Are you still teachable? In what ways are you still learning and growing?

This whole thing of life-long learning should never be taken lightly. You and I need to be continual learners.

A study done by the University of Michigan several years ago found that one-third of all doctors in the US are so busy working that they are 2 years behind on the advancements and breakthroughs in their own fields!

If you are going to be a life-long learner, you have to set aside some time to make the learning process happen in your life.

What is your personal growth plan? Find a good magazine and read it. Buy a good book on a subject of interest to you and devour it. Listen to some great music. Take a course on cooking, or learn to grow a garden.

But be a life-long learner!

Few things bond people together like a shared memory.

Soldiers who battled together, teammates who won a championship, or when work teams hit their goals - they share a connection that never seems to go away. Some memories come as the result of a circumstance, but many memories can be created.

As a leader in your family or your office, why not take the initiative and begin to create some opportunities for some wonderful shared memories. Take some time to plan a trip. Find a reason to have a party. Carve out an excuse to get together with folks to laugh, to share, and to build into other's lives.

The results may be a memory to look back on—and to thank God for.

How are you doing in the area of creativity for your family?

In Genesis 1 it says, "In the beginning, God created..."

As a leader in your family, you may have sensed that things around the household have gotten a little stale from the same old routine. The result is your family may be getting just a little bored with life–and maybe with each other.

Why not today, decide to make something new and positive happen for your family? It will take some planning, but believe me, it will be more than worth it. Imagine putting together a trip (and it doesn't have to be expensive) with your family for a weekend–or maybe just for a day–or an evening. Do some new things together and just watch some new dynamics happen in the life of your family.

That's something a leader should care about.

Sincere Compliments

One of the most fundamental and straightforward ways of winning with other people is to give them a compliment.

Saying words of praise, filled with grace and kindness–and saying them sincerely can go a long way in winning people over...even people who may not have a relationship with God.

John Maxwell says, "A private compliment, turned public, instantly and dramatically increases in value."

Today, where you live and where you work and play, why not compliment the people around you? Words of affirmation go a long way toward helping others in our world where people are hurting and feeling insecure.

Play Like a Yankee

Years ago, a manager for the New York Yankees wanted rookie players to know what a privilege it was to play for the Yankees. He used to tell them, "Boys, it's an honor just to put on the Yankee pinstripes. So, when you put them on, play like world champions. Play like Yankees. Play proud."

When you give someone a reputation to uphold, you give that person something good to shoot for. It's putting something beyond their reach but within their grasp.

Leaders need to constantly remind followers of the importance of conducting themselves with dignity and grace.

If you desire to give others a reputation to uphold–challenge them!

You do them a great favor by challenging them to become something beyond their reach, but in time, something that is within their grasp!

Do you have a high opinion of people—or a low opinion?

The opinions you have about others in your life affect them AND affect you profoundly. A leader at the Harvard Business School said, "People perform consistently as they perceive you expect them to perform."

You see, it really does matter how you treat others.

The Bible talks powerfully about the need to "prefer" others over one's self. A reputation is something that many people spend their entire lives trying to live down or up to. So why not help others up instead of pushing them down? All people, as creations of God, possess both value and potential. You CAN find those things... if you try.

The question is: ARE YOU TRYING?

Compliments and Responsibilities

Part of being a faithful Christ-follower, is backing up your beliefs with actions.

That's especially true with people. It's one thing to tell a teenager that you believe he's a good driver; it's another to let him have the keys to your car for the evening.

It's true in business too. If you want a new manager to rise to the high opinion you've expressed about her, then you have to give her some serious responsibility in the company.

Nothing, I mean nothing, gives people confidence like seeing someone they respect put his money where his mouth is. Not only does it empower them emotionally, but it also resources their drive toward success.

Do you believe in people verbally? That's great. Now back up those words with action.

It is important as leaders to empower those around you.

People become empowered when you provide them with three basic things: opportunity, freedom and security!

I want to create an empowering atmosphere for the leaders who work for me. Giving them opportunities to do new things within the organization, using their own creativity and initiative–and give them the security that I will back them up–even if things don't go as planned.

Empowerment can get tricky sometimes. You have to balance your own needs with the empowered leader's development– and at the same time, keep the best interest of the organization you're leading in mind.

But if you can find that balance and make the proper adjustments, you are well on your way to seeing your leaders not only succeed, but thrive!

MAY

DAY 27

The Rope Principle

When you're trying to empower the folks who work for you, remember the ROPE PRINCIPLE.

Here it is: Give people enough rope to get the job done, but not enough rope to hang themselves! The ROPE PRINCIPLE allows you as a leader to empower your people, but in the process, not do enough damage that it hurts the organization, them, or you!

Some leaders just don't understand this. With the best of intentions, they'll give an emerging leader TOO MUCH ROPE... and disaster sets in. Or, they'll give the leader NO ROPE at all by controlling–the opposite of empowerment. Eventually, the emerging leader gets frustrated and leaves.

How are you leading your people? Through empowerment or through control? The best leaders give just enough rope for their followers to get the job done, but not enough to hang themselves.

Years ago, John Maxwell wrote that he had discovered all employees fall into one of two categories: Salary takers OR Salary makers!

Which one are you? The takers give as little as they can and take their salary. The makers give everything they got and make a contribution far beyond the salary they earn.

As you approach your work, which one of these categories defines you?

"What will I receive" or "what will I give?" "What will it take to get by" or "I'll do whatever it takes to get it right?" "It's not my job" or "whatever the job, can I help you?" "Someone else is responsible" or "I'm responsible?"

What were your answers?

How are you doing in the area of loyalty?

Are you loyal to your church, your pastor, your work, your boss? Loyalty is something that can get lost when we take our eye off of our leaders and start putting the eye on ourselves. Loyal people are increasingly rare–and in demand. Loyal people are committed to a cause greater than themselves and the leaders who are stewards of that cause.

Loyalty to your family, your team, your community, your church, your company, your country... believing the best of them and about them is a great quality that can reward, bring a sense of peace and satisfaction... and honor the Lord.

Where does your loyalty lie?

Great leaders always have great self-discipline–that's without exception.

Unfortunately, our society seeks instant gratification rather than self-discipline. We want instant breakfast, quick cash from ATMs and fast food. But that's not how success in life happens. Neither does the ability to lead. It takes time to be a leader.

Dwight Eisenhower was right when he said, "There are no victories at bargain prices." Self-discipline simply means that an emerging leader must be willing to take the time to learn the ropes, gain from life's losses and disappointments, and just generally, be willing to take the time to pay the price for great leadership.

Do you see leadership as a fast track? Or, do you see it as a disciplined process? Your answer will determine the level of your future influence.

Emotions and time are two particular areas of self-discipline we must look for in potential leaders.

The first is emotions. The second is time. On the emotion side of the equation, leaders have to recognize that their emotional reactions are their own responsibility. A leader is freed when he/she understands that their emotions can't be dictated by other's emotions.

As for time, all of us have the same amount of time every day. But time that is disciplined will allow one to accomplish more, maximize schedules and generally, at the end of the day, have more time for others and self.

Progress comes at a price. So does leadership.

Never underestimate the power or importance of communication.

One study stated that the average American spends 70% of his active hours each day communicating verbally. Without the ability to communicate, a leader cannot effectively cast his vision and call his people to act on that vision.

Everyone who is responsible for teaching the Bible, remember this...a leader is not capable of reaching his/her potential–or challenging others to reach their potential, without effective communication skills.

If you're teaching the Bible somewhere this week to a group of people, will you be interesting or boring? Your ability to communicate will answer that question.

The Value of Nurturing

Do you value "nurturing" your people?

Be it a small group or an office environment, people who are valued and nurtured, can make a big difference in your church or your business.

Here's something key to remember: People cannot be nurtured from a distance or by infrequent, short spurts of attention. They need you to spend time with them–planned time, not just a few words on the way to a meeting.

We live in a fast-paced, demanding world, and time is a difficult thing to give. It's a leader's most valuable commodity. So, when you spend time with someone, it's an investment–and an expression that they are of value to you.

The old adage is true: the man who lives for others has achieved true success.

Believe in Your People

Do you believe in people? Or, are you cynical and mistrusting?

Here's what I believe: When you believe in people, you motivate them and release their potential. People can sense intuitively when someone else believes in them. Anyone can see people as they are. But it takes a leader to see what they can become and encourage them to grow in that direction.

People almost always grow towards a leader's expectations, not his criticisms and examinations. Examinations merely gauge progress. Expectations promote progress. You can hire people to work for you, but you must win their hearts by believing in them in order to have them work with you.

Do you believe in your people? How are you motivating them and promoting progress?

Too many leaders expect their people to encourage themselves.

But most people require outside encouragement to propel them forward. It is vital to their growth. George Adams said that encouragement "is oxygen to the soul."

New leaders need to be encouraged. When they arrive in a new situation, they encounter many changes and undergo many changes themselves.

So, let me encourage you to encourage that new leader in your office or your church. It will help them reach their potential and it will give them energy to go forward—even when they make some mistakes early on in the job.

Whether it is walled cities or giants, obstacles in life can often give God's people either greater faith or an enormous sense of inferiority and frustration.

You see, it's the obstacles in life that can leave us feeling small, insignificant, powerless and afraid. And yet, the obstacles are really small when sized up against the greatness of God!

Good leaders know that it's at these times, when the obstacles seem great—and can make us look small—that it's also the perfect time to make some imperfect decisions, thus mistakes that could be costly.

If you are heading into a solid wall situation, make wise choices, sound decisions, just good common sense decisions, based on firm foundations.

**Become What God
Wants You to Be**

One Bible teacher I know said that the greatest sin of all is to fail to become what God intended us to be.

That really mirrors what happened to Adam in the Garden. Adam failed to become what God, his Creator, designed him to be.

As gas prices rise and the need to conserve energy escalates, keep in mind that the greatest shortage today is not really fuel or electricity–it is the unused potential within our lives to serve God.

God desires for us to discover our potential, and then to dedicate and develop that potential. How are you accomplishing this today?

What's your capacity?

It's hard to predict. Over 50 years ago, Johnny Weissmuller was called the greatest swimmer the world had ever known. Experts said his swimming records would never be broken. He held over 50 records. Today, in swimming competitions across America, 13-year old children are breaking Johnny Weissmuller's records!

It's about capacity. Let me challenge you today to get on your knees and ask God to forgive you for failing to be at your best. Then, get up and discover your potential. Dedicate it to God and develop it for His glory.

My prayer for you today is that someday in the future, you'll be setting all kinds of records–for the glory of God.

In what kind of environment do you live?

That's an important question. Every one of us is a product of the environment that surrounds us. It is no accident that people who tend to be negative are often found in the same household. Two people can live in the same country, under the same law, with the same privileges, and yet turn out to be drastically different in their values, priorities and lifestyles.

Here's the reason why - because their environment, especially at home, was drastically different. Their thoughts simply reflected what they were given by their environment.

So, I ask again—in what kind of environment do you live?

How do you spend your free time?

Now, there is no doubt that Satan will bring his greatest temptations to people when they have time on their hands. It's been said that idle hands are the devil's workshop. That's true of idle time and idle minds too!

As a leader in your home, business or church, let me encourage you to discipline your time and to handle the extra hours you have toward accomplishing something more productive and meaningful.

Fill your free time with tools that will help you think right.

God Hears Our Prayers

No matter what King David did, God always heard his prayers.

David overcame some horrible sins in his life to be close to God. He was a murderer and adulterer and yet he humbled himself before God and confessed his sins.

That allowed David the man, and David the leader, to come closer to God and keep growing in his relationship with God.

David is a great model for us to follow. If God was able to forgive him and build a special relationship with him, then He can do the same with us!

If you are faithful and humble before God, He will draw you close to Him—and hear your prayers!

The Importance of Prayer

Christian leaders need to always remember the importance of prayer on their leadership journey.

Oftentimes, leaders are the recipients of the prayers of followers. But there is an important role of leaders interceding on behalf of others.

Jesus came to this world to talk to people about God. But while on earth, He also talked to God about people. The greatest leader of all-time and eternity prayed for others. In fact, the Bible tells us that He continues to pray for us—interceding on our behalf in the presence of His heavenly Father.

Jesus was a leader. And, Jesus was an intercessor!

Allow Jesus to intercede for you today.

A Fruitful Life

The life of an obedient Christian should be a fruitful life.

That's how God designed us. Jesus chose and appointed us to go and bear fruit that would last and last. The greatest fruit that a leader's life can bear has lasting value.

Great fruit also has compounding value. The seeds of that fruit that is borne multiplies and goes on bearing more and more fruit.

So think of it this way...When you pray for others today, pray that they would be productive and bear fruit–fruit that not only is of value, but also is eternal, compounding in the Kingdom for the glory of God.

As a leader of your family, your business or your ministry, do you pray to have the power of God in your life?

The Apostle Paul prayed that people around him would be strengthened with all power and might—and that this power and might would make them more patient and dependable. That's a good thing to pray for.

God's Holy Spirit can empower us! The Spirit of God can guide us—and prayer can help us and others experience that power. Without the power of God in our lives, we can't make a real difference for Him.

But with His power, you as a leader can bear any burden and face any kind of adversity.

Leaders are highly susceptible to stress.

All of their work is seen by those around them every day. Their decisions have consequences on their employees and their employee's families. Leaders, because they are highly visible, oftentimes find themselves in the proverbial "fishbowl" and subject to criticism and negative comments.

One of the very real ways that Christian leaders can ease the stress of their lives is to increase their time of prayer and intercession.

As smart as a leader may be, they are not smarter than God. As savvy as they may be, they can't touch the wisdom and grace of God.

So, Christian leader, if you want the stress to calm down, raise up the prayer and worship toward Heaven.

Sometimes it's tempting for a leader to experience self-pity and discouragement.

In fact, it's common for some leaders to go through seasons where they sense feelings of inadequacy because they don't feel as though they've been equipped to do the job. Yes, even some of the strongest leaders are tempted by those kinds of thoughts. And if they were to deny that to you–they aren't telling you the truth.

Here's what we know: Leadership is not, nor has it ever been, easy.

If you are a leader and a Christ-follower, remember that it's not just your title that gives you adequacy or worth. Those good things come from a relationship with Jesus Christ–who is your worth, your value, your Savior, your very life!

Would you allow me to take just a moment to encourage you to pray for your pastor and church leaders?

In doing so, you'll be partnering with them in the ministry and giving them protection and empowerment. With your help, they will be able to go places they otherwise could not have gone—or do things they never would have been able to do alone.

And when leaders succeed, so do their followers. Remember Moses when he was in battle with the Amalekites? Well, the same principle of praying for our leaders applies today. Never underestimate the power of prayer for a church leader.

Take a moment today and ask God to give guidance and power to your church leaders.

Adoniram Judson was a 19th Century missionary who was known for his joy in the Lord.

Judson went to Burma in 1812, filled with God's Spirit and a great desire to preach the Gospel. It's said that soon after he arrived, he approached a Burmese business man, and not knowing the language, embraced him.

The man went home and reported to his family that he had seen an angel. The joy of Christ was so radiant in Judson's countenance that people called him "Mr. Glory-Face."

That's the kind of joy that's contagious—and the kind of joy that can make an office, a home, or a church, just about anyplace, very attractive.

So, I ask you leader, how are you doing with joy?

Hey, are you praying for your leaders?

You know, the Bible tells us to do that very thing—to pray for those who are in authority over us—leaders! The only leader in history who didn't need others to pray for him was Jesus. He prayed for Himself, and when God intercedes on behalf of God, no one else is really necessary.

But everyone else, and I mean, everyone else, can benefit from having others pray for them. A pastor who has others praying for him has the potential to go farther than that pastor could ever go alone!

Today, pray for your leaders.

The Influence of Prayer

There's no telling how much the world has changed as the result of the silent prayers of Christians throughout history. Talk about having influence! Charles Spurgeon said: "Whenever God determines to do a great work, He first sets His people to pray." John Wesley said: "God does nothing but in answer to prayer."

The Bible tells us that the effectual and fervent prayer of a person who is right with God will bring about change, comfort and hope. Leaders, especially those leaders who are really gifted and talented, need to remember that with all the gifts and all the talents they possess, the greatest possession they can ever have is the power of God—and that comes through prayer.

Talent Alone is Never Enough

Many leaders today place way too much emphasis on talent and talent alone.

But talent alone is not the secret to success in leadership. If talent alone is enough, then why do you and I know so many talented people who are not successful?

When people achieve great things, others will often explain their accomplishments by simply crediting talent; but talent alone is never the answer. Talent is a wonderful gift from God–and should be celebrated. But in order to move from good to great for God's glory, character and team-building are also essential for success. Talent alone is never enough.

How are you building your character for greatness?

Talented people are gifted by God with their talent.

But talent as a stand-alone trait is not enough for long term success. In the beginning of a task, talent will give you a head start; but the advantage talent gives lasts only a short time.

What separates the talented person from the successful person is hard work, showing up on time, and treating others with respect.

Remember, every one has talent at some level, but values, attitude, and work ethic, behind that talent, will be the difference makers for your success.

Believe in Who You Are

When people figure out their strengths, what often hinders them is not lack of talent, but lack of self confidence.

When people are confident, they unleash capacities from within that almost immediately take them to higher levels.

Whatever your talent, it will not be lifted to its highest level unless you believe in who you are—as someone created in the image of God—or even better than that—someone who has become a child of God.

Believe in your potential. God created you to live above and beyond the average!

A belief is more than an idea that a person possesses. It's an idea that possesses a person. If you want to achieve significantly in life, you must believe you can.

You need to expect to succeed. That doesn't mean you always will–sometimes you'll fail. Mistakes are made.

But if you approach life, especially as a Christ-follower, you need to enter the arena with a passion for victory. And the way to maximize that passion is to maximize your talent and determine to persevere.

Paul said, "I can do all things through Christ who strengthens me."

Today, be strengthened by the passion that God has placed inside of you!

If you want good results, you need to perform good actions. If you want to perform good actions, you must have positive expectations. If you want to have positive expectations, you must first exercise faith and belief.

Paul challenged the Philippian believers to rejoice because of their relationship with Christ. He encouraged them to put into practice the things he had taught them and that they had believed. He reminded them that God would be with them to empower them to do those very things.

Positive expectations come when we exercise faith and belief.

How are you achieving positive expectations in your daily journey?

What is Your Passion in Life?

What makes people take risks, go the extra mile and do whatever it takes to achieve their goals? It isn't talent. It's passion.

Passion is like a fire burning within us. A passionate person never lacks energy. Passionate people refuse to quit, regardless of the circumstances and they make the most of whatever talent they possess.

People who are talented and passionate don't stop until they succeed.

So what is your passion in life? I've met talented people who have passion–and talented people who don't. Which do you think has gone on to make a difference in our world?

Passionate vs. Passionless

What makes a person a passionate leader?

John the Baptist is one of the most passionate people in all of the Bible. And to do what God had called him to do, John NEEDED passion!

John the Baptist, from wardrobe to style of ministry, was a pioneer and every pioneer needs passion. Passion goes a long way in making a difference in life.

Have you ever made a list of people in your life who light passion within you? Or, have you ever made a list of people that snuff out the passion within you? Examine the difference in the list—and strive to become more like the "passionate" and less like the "passionless."

When you have talent and blend that with initiative and focus, you've gone a long way in reaching your goals in life.

Talented people that are lazy and unfocused will continue to be talented, but will also be unemployed and directionless.

Initiative and focus are the one-two punches of taking your talent to new levels of influence and success.

Some talented people just sit and wait until everything is perfect and safe before they act. In all likelihood, they are still talented– and still waiting and waiting and waiting.

Remember this today - when you combine talent, initiative and focus, you have a recipe for success.

Make a Decision

Leaders must be able to make decisions!

It's just not wise to wait until everything is perfect before you take an action. It's better to be 80% sure and make things happen than it is to wait until you are 100% sure. If you wait, you'll probably see the opportunity just pass you by.

Are you waiting to take action on a decision you should be making, a problem you should be resolving, a project you should be starting or a goal you should be reaching? When will you pull the trigger and take action?

Patience is a virtue...and so is making a decision.

Leaders must have the initiative to do the right thing.

When it comes to initiative, there are really only four kinds of people:

People who do the right thing without being told; people who do the right thing when told; people who do the right thing when told more than once; and people who do the right thing, no matter what.

Doing the right thing, no matter what, is the kind of initiative that the best leaders take.

Whether it's your family, your business or your church, take the initiative to do the right thing—and do it at the right time. And then watch what God will do in return.

Talent + Preparation = Success

Achievement follows preparation!

Talent just wants to jump into the action, but preparation positions talent to be highly effective. Talent PLUS preparation often leads to success. On the other hand, talent minus preparation often leads to disaster.

Talent will often provide you with an opportunity for success, but preparation is essential to achieve success.

A famous general in WW II said it this way: "The more you prepare in peace, the less you bleed in war."

How are you preparing your talents today for success tomorrow?

From Anointed to Arrogance

As leaders it is important to remember we are anointed by God and not to become arrogant from our own achievements.

Samson had a record of conflict after conflict. He went from problem to problem. He argued with his parents. His wife was given to his best man. He was deceived by Delilah. He was captured, blinded and enslaved by his enemies.

Samson had such potential as a leader. But he went from being anointed to being arrogant. His was a downward spiral. His problem was <u>inside</u>.

Now let's not kid ourselves. What happened to Samson can happen to us.

If you refuse to take advice, act without thinking, and don't learn from your mistakes, you'll be remembered as the person "who might have been" a great leader.

Are You Approachable?

It is vital as a leader to be approachable.

We've all met people who seemed cold and forbidding, haven't we? And we've all met people who treat us like old friends. The quality of a first time meeting experience depends largely on their approach-ability. People miss many opportunities for connection and the chance to build deep relationships because they simply do not make themselves approachable.

Approachability has little to do with boldness OR timidity. It has EVERYTHING to do with how you conduct yourself and what messages you're sending to others. An approachable leader values people–and appreciates their differences.

So, are you approachable? Sure hope so. People need someone like you to help them on the journey.

The Importance of Friends

Leaders need friends.

Foxholes are usually thought about in connection with warfare. But one doesn't need to be a soldier to understand the importance of friends during tough times... folks who will stand with you when you're under fire.

The power of people sticking together has been appreciated for thousands of years.

Solomon of ancient Israel wrote: "Two are better than one, because they have a good reward for their labor. For if they fall one will lift up his companion, but woe to him who is alone when he falls, for he has no one to help him up."

It's so important to have friends around you in the tough times! Please don't go through that pain alone.

This Independence Day, take a moment to appreciate the people in your life who support you.

Freedom is something that we as leaders should be thankful for always.

We are free to choose our leaders and stand up as leaders, but there are people across this globe that have a very different view of leadership.

There are leaders who are using their power to conduct terror throughout the globe.

Even the continued threat of terrorism on American soil is far too real. We need to be thankful, more than ever, for the freedom we have in this great nation.

This growing threat is a major reason why we need courageous men and women in government to lead us.

Pray for our leaders and for the leaders across the world. And also, on this Independence Day, take a moment to give thanks to God for the leaders who have kept our country safe.

Invest in Things That Last

So many people invest in things that just fade away. Jesus taught that we should invest in things that last.

When it really comes down to it, there is nothing else that really matters in this world more than people and their destiny.

Once you get to know people, you should learn to invest in them. The best relationships are always the result of unselfish giving, not taking. They are relationships that grow... not rust.

Healthy, growing relationships have commitment, communication and concern for others as their signature. Now that's a great investment...an investment that will never fade away.

What are you investing in today?

Beyond Average

EQUIP's founder, John C. Maxwell says: "Average people do not want others to go beyond average."

Man, that's true. And the older you get, the more you understand just how true that statement is.

Mediocrity loves company. It wants no one to succeed. When YOUR friends enjoy great success, let me ask you: Can you genuinely rejoice and celebrate with them? Do you pray for their daily success? This may well be the greatest relationship test of a leader!

Don't be average when your friends perform or are rewarded for an above average effort!

Do you have trouble celebrating the success of others?

The army of Israel under King Saul cowered in fear of Goliath the giant. No one, not even the king would challenge Goliath. Well, David steps up, takes on the giant and he wins.

When word got out about what David did, the women of the country went bonkers over David. They celebrated him and forgot all about King Saul.

And from that day on, Saul resented David and the gifts God had given him.

Hey, don't be jealous over God blessing someone else. It's just not worth it. It speaks of your insecurity.

Change, my friend. Learn to celebrate when others have giant moments.

The high road is always the road less traveled.

It requires thinking and acting in ways that are not natural or common. Those who take the high road become instruments of grace towards others.

High road people understand that what happens to me is not as important as what happens within me. They refuse to let others control their actions.

High road people also commit themselves to travel the high road at all times. As they extend grace to others, they never see themselves as victims, but as recipients of God's grace for a higher purpose.

Today, in what you're facing, are you taking the high road?

One of the key components to successful leadership is to handle relationships well.

If you get the relationship piece right, it's amazing just how much you earn the right to be followed by others. Relational leaders don't assume people will automatically submit to them.

Over time, as the leader demonstrates character, competence and chemistry, people will follow—not because they have to, but because they want to.

Healthy leadership is when leaders use their people skills to earn the right to be followed. Unhealthy leadership just powers up with title and position and forces others to obey.

Sometimes leaders have to play the "because I said so" card. But in most arenas of life, the best leaders earn the right to be followed by building healthy relationships with team members.

How is your relationship component today?

The primary foundation for leadership involves trust and respect.

The silent questions every good follower must ask of a leader are: Do I trust you? Do I respect you?

When people answer "yes" to these two questions, leaders must understand the issue goes even deeper. When leaders dig deeper, they may discover why more people don't follow them. Often a pastor mistakes the love he receives on Sunday. They tell the pastor "Great sermon, Pastor!" However, when times are tough, people may hesitate to support the pastor.

Why? They love the pastor as a friend, but don't support the pastor as a leader. Consequently, they don't commit.

Don't fool yourself into thinking that a title guarantees a following!

It all begins with self-respect.

Once you possess this, you have the capacity to offer genuine respect toward others.

One psychologist said: "Don't always try to be popular. It isn't possible for everyone to like you. It's far more important for you to like yourself. And when you respect yourself, strangely, you get more respect than if you court it from others."

Hey, understand who you are and how God made you. Appreciate the gifts God's given you. Do your work well and don't take criticism personally. And, if you'll just start by treating others as though they were important, you'll be amazed at how showing them respect will earn respect back toward you.

If your leader at work expects more from you than others have in the past, don't criticize that; celebrate it!

Good leaders raise the bar. They lead the way in requiring the team to perform with excellence. They push for improvement and they just refuse to "get by."

Jesus spoke of this kind of personal growth when He taught His disciples to go the extra mile, to give others your coat not just your shirt, and to turn the other cheek when hit.

Today, thank God for a boss, a parent, a coach who sets high personal standards for you. You see, the best leaders build respect through keeping the bar high!

Strong Convictions Precede Great Actions

Strong convictions precede great actions.

Leaders understand that if they submit to pressure from peers, they move DOWN to their level. If they stand up for beliefs, they invite others to that higher level. If you move with the crowd, you'll get no further than the crowd.

Now, think about it...if 40 million people had a really bad idea, it's still a bad idea even though there are so many who support the bad idea.

A good leader knows not only what's right, but when to take a stand.

Remember, you can't be an effective leader if you don't know what you believe. Strong convictions precede great actions.

Have you ever been exposed to a leader who possesses a maturity well beyond their age and experience?

When a leader does that, they win the confidence and respect of people. The marks of maturity include responsibility. Maturity doesn't come with age, it comes with accepting responsibility. The marks of maturity also include security. People look for security, and a secure environment is provided by a secure leader!

What marks of maturity do you display? Are you responsible? Secure? Hey, irresponsible and insecure leaders are immature leaders!

Ask God today to help you on your leadership journey to be responsible in your actions and secure in your relationships.

The way leaders view the world reflects their heart.

A traveler nearing a city asked an old man by the roadside, "What are people like in this city?"

The old man said, "What were they like where you came from?"

"Horrible" said the traveler.

The old man said, "You will find them the same in the city ahead."

Later that same day, another traveler stopped and asked the old man the same question. The old man replied like before, "What were they like where you came from?"

The second traveler said, "They were great! Very friendly!"

The old man responded, "That's exactly how you will find the people there."

The old man was very wise. He knew that the way the men saw others was a reflection of the men themselves.

How are you viewing others?

Many consider King David the greatest king in the history of Israel. David, as great as he was though, failed to practice the MIRROR PRINCIPLE.

That's examining ourselves before we examine others. David's neglect became *sin* which became *more sin*. And sadly, as his sins accelerated, he was blind to his need of repentance. His sin of adultery led him to conspiracy, then to murder.

It was a member of his inner-circle, Nathan, who confronted David about his sin and began to take steps for him to get out of the mess he had made. David abused power at the highest levels of his country's government and His God's commandments.

As you start your day, before you lead others, maybe you should first take a look in the mirror. I know I do.

It doesn't take a psychiatrist to see that many people are hurting today.

So many people are lonely; damaged emotionally and physically. They are needy souls crying out for help. Leaders understand that often when people attack or criticize them, they are actually displaying their own hurt. Like a wild animal backed in to a corner, they lash out in fear and anger over their own pain.

Unfortunately, leaders are the ones who often get blamed for this pain...since they are the ones responsible for the organization or know the details of their critics' pain and woundedness. When a leader gets criticized, sometimes it has merit.

However, it's always a good idea for you to take a look at the person doing the criticizing–because hurt people hurt people.

Live Outside Yourself

Albert Einstein said that, "a person first starts to live when he can live outside of himself."

Most people, including leaders, have a difficult time living outside of their own little world. Christian leaders can hide behind the excuse that they are doing God's work. Unfortunately, this can be a disguise for selfishness. The fact is, we are concerned about it because it is what WE are doing at the moment.

Let's get some perspective, my friend. See the big-picture of life, not just your own self-interests. Break out of the mold of focusing on yourself and take a lesson from the Lord Jesus who said, "Do unto others as you would have them do unto you."

Success can bring many things: power, privilege, fame, wealth.

Sadly, as many leaders rise in their position, they become forgetful of the place they came from. As we travel the world, our EQUIP team has observed many leaders that abuse those under them. Leadership for some has become a power trip. And that just isn't a Biblical model.

Jesus was born in a barn. He grew up in a backwater town called Nazareth. He owned no property–and the only clothes he owned he wore every day. Jesus put Himself in the place of others. He walked where they walked–he suffered what they suffered. He spoke their language and identified with their needs. Jesus was the ultimate servant leader.

Are you a servant leader?

Have a Teachable Spirit

Effective leaders never stop growing.

Whether they continue learning or not has to do with not only who is teaching them—but even more with how teachable they are.

We can learn from anyone—good or bad. The fact is we can learn in unlikely places—and from unlikely people. However, only a TEACHABLE spirit will allow us to capitalize on this reality.

Here's how to learn from others: Value people. Identify with people's strengths and weaknesses. And, ask questions. When you observe people or interact with people, do you have a desire to learn from them?

Always remember: Each person we meet has the potential to teach us something!

JUL

DAY 21

Focus on Others

Dale Carnegie was right: He said, "You can make more friends in two months by becoming interested in other people than you can in two years by trying to get other people interested in you."

The idea is simple: If you want to connect with others, focus on them not on yourself. That's what CHARISMA is all about.

Keep this in mind: People are interested in the person who is interested in them. People don't care how much you know until they know how much you care. For leaders, these concepts come to life through listening and having an inquiring mind... all with the motivation to add value to others.

Are you focused on others?

People generally respond to the expectations they sense a leader has of them.

In other words, they will live up or down to the expectations they believe a leader has of them. This is why we must believe the best about everyone we lead.

Everyone has the potential to become the person God intended them to be. It often takes a leader, however, to bring out the best in those people.

Barnabas in the Bible was such a leader. He was an enormous encourager. He saw potential in people that others didn't see. What a great role model!

Today, look for the best in people and just watch how they respond.

Leaders understand that within their roles and responsibilities comes confrontation.

Few leaders enjoy it, but nevertheless, it comes with the territory of leading others. If a confrontation is on the horizon where you're leading, try to make it a positive experience in that person's life.

Conflict is inevitable. The way to make it more bearable is to make sure you demonstrate love before and during the actual confrontation. You see, caring for people precedes confronting people.

As you lay out the issues, bathe your words in love and power; and encourage the person you're confronting that they can get better–and that they can do better.

Obedience to God is so important!

Joshua and Caleb were obedient and because of it, they were allowed to enter into the promise land. But for leaders, obedience is a part, but not the whole. You see, if leaders can't take others with them on their God-given trip, they fail in their God-given mission.

Leadership is influence. Joshua came face to face with the true nature of leadership when he failed to influence the people to do what they should have done alone.

Question: What are you currently doing to increase your influence? And while you continue to obey God about the mission, what are you doing to influence others to take the journey with you?

Leaders should always desire to become better.

Many people who experience ineffectiveness as leaders give up and never try to lead again. Fortunately for the children of Israel, Joshua wasn't that type of person. He desired to become a better leader. And that's a good thing.

Joshua would later receive a second chance in his leadership. And during the interim, he continued to be faithful to God and to learn as much as he could from Moses, who would become his mentor.

Maybe today you really blew it as a leader. Are you listening? And you're thinking you'll give up and never try to lead again. Hey, get up, dust yourself off and wait for God to open another door.

Leader's Influence vs. People's Resistance

A leader's influence must be greater than the people's resistance.

That is especially important when the people face a formidable challenge or extremely difficult circumstance.

Andy Stanley puts it this way: "You can't resist the will of God and receive the grace of God at the same time." Great point!

In the case of Joshua in the Bible, the people's resistance was huge and his influence was comparatively small.

But in time, God asked Joshua to gain in influence and lead the people beyond the time of Moses. It takes time to build influence. For Joshua–it took FORTY YEARS! But what was the rush? In those four decades God prepared Joshua to lead the children of Israel through some remarkable moments–and great glory!

Do you feel any resistance today? Ask God for greater influence!

As leaders, we must obey the Lord like Joshua did.

Joshua was a man of prayer. When Moses returned to camp following his times with God, Joshua stayed close to the tabernacle of worship. Joshua didn't try to ride on Moses' coattails when it came to his own need for spiritual direction. And, as Joshua knew the mind of God, he was able to obey the will of God.

Oswald Chambers said it like this: "Never try to explain God until you have obeyed him. The only part of God we understand is the part we have obeyed."

Wow, that's good!

Joshua obeyed God...when he was a servant, a warrior and a leader. Obedience consumed him. And obedience rewarded him.

So, how's your walk with God?

A leader's legacy is found in his family.

Jonathan Edwards was one of the most gifted and influential leaders of the 18th century in America. Edwards, a gifted preacher and scholar, and his wife Sarah left an incredible family legacy based on their influence:

13 college presidents, 75 college professors, 100 lawyers, 30 judges, 66 physicians, 80 public office holders, 3 US Senators, 3 mayors of major cities, and 1 Vice President. Wow!

Now, if you want to impact your community and change your world, the place to start is your home.

Hey leader, are you placing your family in the column of things that matter most in life? If you don't know where you stand with your family, ask them.

Becoming a leader is a lot like investing successfully in the stock market. If your hope is to make a fortune in one day, you're not going to be successful. What matters most is what you do day by day over the long haul.

One leader put it this way: "The secret of our success is found in our *daily agenda.*"

If you continually invest in your leadership development, letting your assets compound, the inevitable results will be grown over time.

Leadership ability is not static. No matter where you are on your leadership radar today, you can get better at leadership tomorrow!

What is your agenda for today?

Leadership Takes Time

Although it's true that some people are born with greater natural gifts than others, the ability to lead is really a collection of skills, nearly all of which can be improved or learned.

But that process doesn't happen overnight. Leadership is complicated. It has so many facets: there's respect, experience, emotional strength, people skills, vision, timing...and the list goes on and on.

Leaders require seasoning to become effective leaders. In short, the best leaders start out in the stock room taking inventory... not working the floor with customers and definitely not managing the shop.

Leadership takes time.

So, don't get in a hurry. Enjoy where God has you right now. Learn and grow!

Before God could use Joseph to the maximum, he had to take him through the minimum. Joseph had to be prepared for leadership.

He had to be purified and tested, even forged into the leader he had the potential to become.

Like a lot of young leaders Joseph had a vision long on greatness but short on experience to make that vision come true. So, God took him on a journey that allowed Joseph to become the man, the leader, He intended for Joseph to be.

The next time you get impatient about where you are on the leadership journey, remember, Joseph needed time to mature. And maybe that's true with you too. Hang in there!

There is a learning process for all leaders. Just about everyone starts out in leadership with a state of ignorance.

That's where Joseph in the Bible began. He didn't understand the dynamics of his family. He was ignorant of how his brothers would react when he shared his big dreams about how God was going to use him in a big way.

The Scriptures say his brothers already hated him before he shared his dream. And when he shared...they hated him even more. Joseph didn't know what he was doing in those younger years. And he didn't know what he didn't know!

Out of ignorance and inexperience he unnecessarily alienated his family for more than 20 years.

A word of caution to young leaders: Admit that there are some things about leadership you don't know. Find a mentor...and learn.

Leadership is Difficult

No one has ever said leadership is easy.

It took a life changing incident for Joseph to understand this point, but it worked. It got Joseph's attention and started him on the road to change. As a slave in Egypt, he began to learn about what he didn't know. He came to understand that leadership is difficult and carries a huge weight of responsibility.

Over the years, Joseph experienced betrayal, and he received lessons in human nature, relationships, and leadership. The process molded his character. He developed patience and humility. And he began to recognize that God was his source of blessing and power.

Are you facing difficulties today? Remember God is your source of power!

Leaders who show great skill when opportunity presents itself, do so only because they've paid the price to prepare for that opportunity.

When Joseph was finally called before Pharoah, he performed with excellence and with wisdom. He didn't succeed because he suddenly got good at age thirty. He succeeded because he had been paying the price for 13 years.

Because of his wisdom and discernment, Joseph was made second in command, in what was the most powerful nation on earth. Joseph grew as a leader and it started to show.

Eventually, all the world would know of Joseph's leadership.

How are you preparing today for your opportunity later on?

Often times, as leaders, past pains can be building blocks for what God has in store!

For 7 years, during a time of plenty for Egypt, Joseph skillfully executed his leadership plan. He filled the cities of Egypt with grain, and he prepared the country for a coming famine. His previous years of pain and growth were paying off now in a big-time way.

But you can really see how far his leadership had come by observing what he did during the lean years that followed. His economic plan not only fed his nation during famine, but surrounding nations as well.

In a few short years, he was able to acquire just about all the remaining wealth in the regions beyond Egypt and deliver those assets to his boss.

Let this be encouragement to you today: The pains of your past will someday bring gain for the future.

Get Bitter or Get Better!

The larger the task before us, the greater the trials! When faced with trials, people either get bitter or better.

Joseph chose to get better.

He had plenty of opportunities to become negative. He could have held a grudge against so many individuals: his brothers, the slave traders, Potiphar's wife, and the chief butler.

But instead, he just let all of that go. He turned to God in the midst of his struggle and viewed those who had offended him in the past as instruments of God's divine sovereignty.

The Bible says in James 5: "You also be patient...like Job...the Lord is compassionate and merciful."

That's a great promise when the trials start coming.

Samuel was a leader who welcomed transition.

As a judge over Israel, Samuel was a very visible leader. Yet, Samuel gave his military and civil authority over to Saul at God's direction–with no questions asked. That was the beginning of a season where Samuel not only transitioned power over to Saul, but Samuel began to publicly honor Saul.

Samuel did what Promise Keeper's Founder Bill McCartney expressed a few years ago: "We are not here," he said, "to compete with each other, but to complete each other."

Is God leading you to hand off some of your leadership responsibilities? Well, go ahead and start the process. You'll be glad you did.

Be Trustworthy

When you don't trust a leader, you can't follow.

Have you ever started strong and finished weak? Well, if you have, you can somewhat identify with the story of Samson. Never has there been a leader with so much potential– and so much disappointment.

Samson had everything going for him; the right pedigree; supportive family... and the Spirit of God was upon him. But Samson, in a 20-year-period, just messed up in a big-time way.

Oh, he got off to a good start, but then he made some dumb decisions and hung around the wrong people until one day, he had lost his power and his influence.

Samson came short of what he could have been because he lacked character. You just couldn't trust the guy... and it destroyed his career.

Be trustworthy, my friend. If you're not, it'll cost you.

Some people think that their private imperfections won't have public consequences, but they almost always do. Leaders cannot escape who they truly are, and what they do in the dark is often exposed in the light.

If what they do is good, it builds character in the leader and trust in the people. If what they do is bad, then it undermines everything they do until there is no solid ground left for them to stand on.

Look, no leader today is absent of imperfections. However, if the leader ignores them or pretends to think they have an exemption from sin, that's a problem!

Leader: Is there any sign of trouble present in your life that you're ignoring or discounting? If "yes"–get some help so you won't be a train wreck in the Kingdom of God.

A leader must have the respect of their people.

You know, we don't know a whole lot about Deborah in the Bible. We do know she was a judge in Israel—and we do know that during her administration she had huge influence.

In a day and culture when men were atop the leadership ladder, Deborah carved out a place in history. Deborah not only had influence over the citizens of Israel, she also had their respect.

When leaders have influence, people begin to follow them. When they have respect, the people keep following them.

Here's something all of us need to remember: When a leader gains respect, leading becomes easier.

How in the world did a woman gain respect in a male dominated culture, in ancient Israel, around 1100 B.C.?

How did this woman, her name Deborah, come to be one of the greatest leaders of her generation? She did it the same way any man or woman would do it today—she gained the respect of the people she led.

Gaining the respect of others always begins with having respect for yourself. And, gaining respect involves that of being a principled person... a person who stands firm on their convictions.

What are you relying on for people to respect you? Your title? Your position? Well, your reliance on these may cause you to wait awhile for respect to come your way.

Remember leader: respect is earned and takes time to get.

The little engine that made it, did so not because he had more power or skills. The little engine made it because he *thought* he could.

The little engine had more *confidence*.

Many times we feel little - like little insignificant engines. But if we hone our skills and talents, then add a good dose of confidence, we can climb hills and overcome obstacles and barriers that could have stopped us dead in our tracks.

Here is a question: Why pull off the track and stop when you can conquer those mountains with the momentum of confidence in your engine?

The Big Mo

There's nothing like momentum to move an organization or a movement forward.

The largest locomotive in the New York Central System, while standing still, can be prevented from moving by a single one inch block of wood placed in front of each of the eight drive wheels! The same locomotive moving at 100mph can crash through a wall of steel reinforced concrete five feet thick.

The only difference is momentum.

Confidence gives leaders the momentum to make the difference. Low confidence equals little momentum. High confidence can give you the momentum to become the person God wants you to be.

Today, how will you build momentum?

Confidence cannot and should not replace character or skill or knowledge. After all, these are some of the foundational aspects of a leader's life.

But confidence does enhance these qualities so that you can be a person who makes a difference. When you have knowledge or skill and the momentum that confidence brings, then things begin to happen in your relationships.

Jesus Christ has made his strength and confidence available to you. As you continue to shape your life, remember his confidence can live in you and work through you and into the lives of the people you know and influence.

Confidence because of–and through–Jesus Christ is a wonderful thing.

How is your confidence?

Don't be a Lone Ranger!

It's never healthy to be a Lone Ranger in life.

When we design our lives after the Lone Ranger concept, we are sure to suffer some unfavorable consequences. We develop a distorted perception of ourselves, our ministries and other people.

We are imbalanced and incomplete without the other members of the Body of Christ. We become irrelevant because we don't live where other people live.

There is a sense of exclusiveness and an inability to relate to the real world.

So if I'm talking to the Lone Ranger Leader, be warned my friend...that's a very distorted and dysfunctional way to lead. And you need to change.

Take Advantage of Opportunities

Have you ever met anyone who believes that success comes from taking advantage of opportunities?

There is some truth in that, but it's rather one-dimensional. The problem with folks believing success is just taking advantage of opportunities, often spend a great deal of their time regretting "lost" opportunities.

These are the "if only" folks. "If only my boss would give me a chance; If only my wife would...if only my church would..."

You get the idea. Look, if all we do is wait for opportunities to come our way, we won't be ready when it comes.

Listen, if your ship came in tomorrow morning, what in the world would you do with it? You don't even have a harbor to anchor it.

So get busy today planning for tomorrow's opportunities. Don't wait!

It's been said that people live in either one of two tents: Content or Discontent.

In which tent do you live?

The contented person looks beyond circumstances and sees a better day. The discontented person looks AT circumstances and sees no other way.

The contented person understands the purpose for which he or she was born; the discontented person looks at others' success with a face full of scorn.

All persons live in one of two tents–content or discontent.

In which tent do you live?

Problems are Predictors

Problems are predictors.

They forecast the future by exposing the trends of today. How you react to difficulty when it begins to surface will determine where you and the problem will be tomorrow. No trail will leave you tomorrow where you are today.

The decisions we make today concerning problems we have will shape our future.

Remember this: The circumstances we find ourselves in today are a direct reflection of the decisions we made yesterday. Problems really are predictors.

If you see the negative trends of today, it will give you insight into the problems you might have tomorrow.

Problems are everywhere! Problems, problems, problems.

Everywhere you look, there are problems. Problems don't respect anyone, any place or any time. Sooner or later a person, if he or she is wise, discovers that life is a good mixture of good and bad days, victory and defeat, give and take. That's life!

The person who loses their temper in the midst of problems usually loses out. That's the person that takes themselves just too seriously. Problems have always been and always will be.

What matters most is how we respond to problems...positively or negatively. That's what matters most.

How are you responding to problems?

Problems are like a weather forecast.

They tell you what the environment is going to be like down the road by a day or two. Problems are indicators which measure progress and development. They are communicators letting us know vital information. Sometimes, problems yell for attention or point for redirection.

Here's what we know. Problems can never be ignored. If you sit back and analyze every problem, you can recognize the message the problem is sending.

So, if you want to know what the forecast will be at home or the office in the next few days, just take a look at today's problem.

How Are You Defined?

What is a leader defined by?

Have you ever known someone who could walk into a room full of people and in a few short minutes completely change the atmosphere of that room? Or, how about that person who keeps their head above water while everyone else seems to be drowning in confusion? What about the person who smiles when others are critical and snarling?

These are the kind of people Christ-followers should be: People who have learned to live their lives based upon what is right and not what is easy.

These are folks who face each day with joy and optimism. These are people who work while others worry.

What about you? How are you defined? Smiling or snarling, in life?

Some give to live while other people live to give.

Each has its own philosophy of life. A person who gives to live will never do something for anyone without expecting a reward. They keep a record of what they give. But a person who lives to give never expects any recognition or reward. This is a person who gives but doesn't expect anything in return.

The person who gives to live says, "HOW MUCH DO I HAVE TO GIVE?" But the person who lives to give says, "HOW MUCH MORE IS NEEDED TO MEET THE NEED?"

See the difference? The Christian life is saturated by giving...by living to give.

Are you living to give?

Don't Live the Life of a Loner

This world is just too large and complex to live the life of a loner.

A 10-year-old boy was selling pencils door to door. When an interested adult at one house asked him the reason for selling pencils, he said, "I WANT TO RAISE 6 MILLION DOLLARS TO BUILD A NEW HOSPITAL FOR THE CITY."

The adult neighbor was shocked. "That's a mighty big dream for such a small boy, isn't it?" The boy said, "No. I have a friend who's helping me!"

You and I need each other. We need one another in the Body of Christ.

Today I encourage you to like others and... make yourself more likeable. It's a great way to go through life—with friends who share your values and your dreams.

With all the rising fuel costs around us, we all grieve over wasted energy.

But the greatest waste of energy may be found far beyond less than fuel efficient means: It's the waste of unused potential in people's lives.

It's stated that the average person uses only about 10% of his or her potential. What would happen if we could raise that person's potential another 15 or 20%? Could be interesting!

Failing to become all God designed you and me to be seems like a sin. It's failing to trust God to teach us more, show us more, equip us more, relate to more, respond to more, love more, help more and share more. As we try not to waste fuel these days, let's not waste our potential for God's glory either!

Are you trusting God with your leadership potential?

AUG

DAY 24

Don't Be A Quitter!

There are lots of people who quit...and they tend to want to encourage others to quit.

History is full of all kinds of folks who were advised to quit just short of their great accomplishment. Benjamin Franklin was told to quit the foolish work he was doing with lightning and electricity. So were Christopher Columbus and the Wright Brothers, and Thomas Edison and Abraham Lincoln. And, and, and...!

However, these and others didn't quit. They pressed on, gave it their very best and as a consequence not only accomplished their dream, but they made other people's lives better.

Today, don't quit. You've only just begun!

An old carpenter gave this advice to a young apprentice: "Measure twice and saw once."

That's a great word for builders of houses and builders of lives. The plans established for any endeavor should be thought through and well-planned.

Counting the cost before we enter into a venture is something Jesus Christ taught us to do. Measuring, planning and organizing are great virtues when put into practice in business, church work, or at home. I know I have had to saw twice because I measured only once in my lifetime—in short, I didn't plan it out or think it through.

Maybe you know a little bit about sawing and measuring that you could share right now.

Spend Time with Encouragers

You can trace your successes and failures in life to your most significant relationships!

Surround yourself with people who add value to you and encourage you, and your talent will go in a positive direction. Spend time with folks who constantly drain you, pull you in the wrong direction or try to knock you down, and it will be almost impossible for your talent to reach its highest potential.

Almost all our sorrows can be traced to relationships with the wrong people and joys to relationships with the right people. Relationships in our lives really do make or break us. They either lift us up or take us down.

Today, make time to spend time with encouragers–people who will lift you up!

Friendships are like bank accounts. You cannot continue to draw on them without making deposits.

If either of you become permanently overdrawn, the relationship won't last. Solid relationships must be beneficial to both parties. Each person has to put the other first, but both must have benefit. Relationships that continue to be one-sided will not remain solid.

If you desire to become a talent-plus person in the area of relationships–a person whose relationships influence him or her in a positive direction–there are some important steps to take.

The first step is to identify the most important people in your life and spend time with people whose opinion you value the most.

John Maxwell states that "One is too small a number to achieve greatness."

He's right. If you want to accomplish anything that makes a major difference, then do it as a part of a team. Teamwork not only allows a person to do what he couldn't otherwise do; it also has a compounding effect on all he possesses, including his talent.

If you believe one person is a work of God, then a group of talented people working together is a work of art!

Whatever your vision or desire, TEAMWORK MAKES THE DREAM WORK!

All talented people have a choice to make—do their own thing and get all the credit, or do the team thing and share the credit, and give glory to God.

Talented people accomplish more when working with others and are also more fulfilled than those who go it alone.

Here's what I know: Trying to accomplish a big task alone is the slowest and blandest of journeys.

If it is your desire to choose teamwork over solo effort, then do the following: GIVE THE CREDIT FOR SUCCESS TO THE TEAM!

Jesus recruited and mentored the most important team ever assembled.

His team would launch His church on the journey to fulfill his Great Commission. He chose specific people for specific roles.

In Mark 2, we read about how Jesus called Matthew, the tax collector, to his team. He seemed an odd choice, but Jesus was never bound by human opinion.

You and I must learn how to find team members with the highest potential to embrace the dream and help move the dream to reality. They need to be faithful, available, have initiative and be hungry to learn. That's what makes team players so special.

Who are your team members?

Are you a good team player?

Do your goals primarily benefit you or your team? If you think everything is about you, you will never be a good team player.

The best team players add value to other players on the team. They help their teammates reach their highest potential. And when you work with great teammates long enough, they will begin to compound team success, and ultimately your success. The best team players, like the best of Jesus' disciples, understood that it was all about Jesus and the team, not just about themselves.

Today, ask yourself: Are you focused on the team or on yourself?

**Talent Alone Isn't
the Secret to Success**

Many leaders today place too much emphasis on talent alone. Well, talent alone is not the secret to success.

After all, how many talented people do we know that haven't experienced success and probably never will?

When people achieve great things, people will try to explain it by talking about their talent. But they don't spend much time talking about how they developed their talent or matched an excellent attitude with their excellent talent.

Talent is never enough–and when we understand that, we begin a journey of success.

Think about this today: How is your attitude and development building your talent for success?

A leader must show courage daily.

People think of courage as a quality required only in times of extreme danger or stress, such as war or disaster. It's much larger than that. Courage is an everyday virtue that is essential every time we are tested.

To discover, develop and use our talent, we need courage. A great deal of talent is wasted because of a lack of courage. On the other hand, if we display courage, our courage will be tested.

If you desire to become a more courageous person today, start by doing the right things instead of the convenient things. That's a huge first step toward having a brave heart.

Be Courageous!

David is a perfect example of a leader who was courageous!

King Saul and his army were dismayed and greatly afraid in the face of Goliath. When David visited his older brothers who were soldiers in Saul's army, he volunteered to fight the giant!

And how would he defeat the mighty Goliath and transform the cowardly army into a winning army? COURAGE!

Because of his courage, David acted differently from King Saul, his brothers and the soldiers. Courage can make a difference for you and in you as you face giant obstacles this day.

Facing a giant task today? Face it courageously!

Labor Day Weekend is that time when we give special attention to the millions across this land who make up the nation's mighty workforce.

There's no doubt that having a job is an important part of our lives, our worth—even our self-esteem. When unemployment is up, the national mood is up. When it's down, so is the national mood.

In the book of Genesis, labor came about because of Adam's sin. But God is in the business of turning curses into crowns.

Today, work is respected—and absolutely necessary. Work gives dignity to the worker and glory to God.

Go to work today with the feeling of confidence that only God can give.

Leaders Must be Humble

Leaders must strive to show humility.

The Apostle Paul was a leader with tremendous strength and courage.

It's interesting to note his comments about his weaknesses in I Corinthians 2. Paul knew he was tempted by pride. In fact, pride was a big, big thing for Paul.

And it's a big, big thing for us.

Leaders must serve in humility. They need to be dependent on God and never seek the glory that only God deserves.

In fact, God gives grace to the humble–and if there was ever a category of people who needed God's grace in abundance, it is leaders.

Humble yourself today and give all the glory back to Him!

Work is important!

If you have never given serious consideration to the importance of work in our culture, think about this: Our 24 hour days are sliced into 10 hours of working, 8 hours of sleeping and about 6 hours of leisure.

So the greatest portion of our day is work—and going to and from work!

Consider something else: When you meet someone, after they tell you who they are, how long is it until you ask, "What do you do?"

A casual approach to the workplace isn't a great life-plan. This is where we spend so much time; therefore, how we approach our work can define us. You see, what we do really does matter in this world.

Work matters! Labor is a big part of who we are.

Does your job reflect who you are?

Our nation is built upon workers.

Every year, this country requires thousands of new engineers, nurses, mechanics, farmers and sales personnel to fill job openings within the economy. It is the labor of these kinds of men and women who bring great prosperity to our nation.

Work began in the Bible as a curse. But God in his grace has turned work into a blessing.

Today, if you are a part of this nation's workforce, thank you for all that you are doing to keep this nation's economy competitive in an ever changing world.

May God bless you and give you strength as you serve Him—in your work!

Some people have little respect for an honest day's work.

There is a sign on the entrance of a great manufacturing plant which reads like this: "IF YOU ARE LIKE A WHEELBARROW, GOING NO FARTHER THAN YOU ARE PUSHED, YOU NEED NOT APPLY HERE!"

Many people need to be pushed. Someone said "There are 3 kinds of people in the world: Those who MAKE things happen. Those who WATCH things happen. And those who say, 'WHAT HAPPENED?'"

In the workplace today, which kind of person will you be?

Ecclesiastes says, "Whatsoever your hand finds to do, do it with all your might." God wants us to work–honestly and earnestly!

So, we have set aside Labor Day to honor millions of people who work hard–people who work with their hands with all of their might.

And maybe from your work this day, you're really tired.

And to you, the tired worker, Jesus says, "Come to me–you who labor and are heavy laden and I will give you rest."

As we remember Labor Day Weekend, let's also remember Jesus Christ's invitation to you to rest in Him–and the promise that in Him, you will find rest.

Making Right Decisions

Personal growth is vital to your leadership.

If you cease to grow, you cease to be a healthy leader. Healthy things naturally grow. To grow personally requires you to seize the opportunities daily. Each day–you must determine how you can grow as a leader.

Ben Franklin said: "One today is worth two tomorrows; what I am to be, I am becoming." It's true. You will become what you are becoming right now. Remember this:

Successful people make right decisions early–and manage those decisions daily.

What right decisions are you doing today to build for your tomorrow?

Time is Priceless

Your time—and my time—well, our time, is priceless.

Someone wisely noted that time is more valuable than money. You can always get more money, but you cannot get more time.

Ralph Waldo Emerson said: "Guard well your spare moments. They are like uncut diamonds. Discard them and their value will never be known. Improve them and they can become your brightest gems."

The way I use my time to establish my daily priorities really does matter. We may not be able to change time, but we can change our priorities to maximize our time.

After all, your time—my time—our time, is priceless!

How are you planning your day to best prioritize your priceless time?

Become Better at Life

How do we create a better life?

If you want a better world, composed of better nations, inhabited by better states, filled with better counties, made up of better cities, comprised of better neighborhoods, illuminated by better churches, populated by better families, then here's what you have to do: YOU have to become a better person.

The way we become better at life is a mixture of faith in God and His Son Jesus Christ, and by working on our leadership skills.

Before we can ever change or lead the world, we first need to change and lead ourselves. Self- leadership is the first step in being a difference-maker in our world.

How are you becoming a better person today?

All organizations that continue to grow, including your church, have one thing in common: They have a leader who is personally growing!

In Colossians 2, Paul speaks to Christ followers; that we should walk in Christ, be rooted and built up in Christ, be teachable and be thankful!

Not one of those actions is easy or automatic. They require a great degree of management. And all require SELF leadership.

Remember leader, managing your personal growth requires you to lead yourself first before you're qualified to ever lead others!

As a leader, you have a responsibility to be God's steward on earth.

God wants to use you as a vehicle to bring glory to Himself.

Whatever He gives you in terms of resources is to be channeled to others, not jammed up and stored for personal benefit. The more open you are, the more blessed you will be and the more of His grace will flow out to the world around you.

And no matter how much you pass on, there will always be more available.

How "open" would you say you've been as a channel of God's love, grace and power? What can you do today to increase that openness?

Money does talk.

Money tells an individual how valuable he is to whoever pays his salary. Pay for leadership and get leaders. Pay peanuts and you get monkeys.

There was a clothing manufacturer who turned out thousands of sweatshirts that said on the front, "Money Isn't Everything." He went bankrupt.

Now money isn't the only way to show appreciation for a job well done, but it's one of the best ways. If you're one of those folks who take pride in how little you're paying your people, you need a therapist. Get a life.

A scarcity mentality like yours will create on organization filled with resentment and anger.

Pay your people well!!

You probably know the story of the Good Samaritan.

A business traveler is mugged and robbed. The robbers saw the targeted man as a victim to exploit. When religious leaders came by and walked around the bleeding man, they saw him as a problem to avoid. When the Samaritan saw the man, he saw him as a person to help.

When you see people who are wounded and hurting all around you, how do you *really* see them?

Do you see them as victims to exploit or to take advantage of? Or, do you see them as problems to avoid? Or like the Samaritan, do you see them as people who need your help?

Be a good Samaritan leader today, see a need and help!

When you realize that people treat you according to how they see themselves rather than how you really are, you are less likely to be affected by their behavior.

Your self-image will reflect who you are, not how you're treated by others. You will not be riding an emotional roller coaster.

This type of stability will have an enormous effect on how you feel toward and deal with others. It really gets down to responsibility.

I am responsible for how I treat others. I may not be responsible for how they treat me, but I am responsible for my reaction to those who are difficult.

Remember, you can't choose how others will treat you, but you can choose how you will treat others.

Criticism!

We don't like it, but a leader's ability to take criticism can make us or break us. No one is indifferent to criticism. It causes us to respond either positively or negatively.

Learning how to handle criticism is one of the most difficult things a leader can experience. But leaders are highly subject to criticism. When you are criticized, take the positive approach.

If you are doing something, making a difference, adding value to others, guess what? You'll be criticized. When you stick your neck out someone will want to chop it off! If you think your critics are sharpening their knives, congratulations!

But make sure your response is positive and with patience.

You're leading. And criticism goes with the job.

Constructive vs. Destructive Criticism

There is a BIG difference between constructive criticism and destructive criticism. And leaders need to know the difference.

When criticized, ask yourself, what is the spirit of the criticism? Also ask, when was the criticism given? Then ask, why was the criticism given?

Sometimes the person who is experiencing difficulties and problems will deal with others in a negative, critical way.

Constructive criticism is done *privately*, not publicly. It's done to *build up*, not to tear down.

Someone got it wrong when they said, tongue-in-cheek, "Constructive criticism is when I criticize you; destructive criticism is when you criticize me."

Well, not really. Constructive criticism tries to *help me*. Destructive criticism tries to *hurt me*.

Strive to be a constructive leader, not destructive.

Living a Different Value System

Good people get criticized!

No one had purer motives to help people than Jesus Christ. But his critics called him a glutton, a drunkard, and a friend of sinners. If our lives are Christ-like, we can *expect* criticism.

In fact, there are times when we should see criticism from the world around us as an endorsement that our lives have been changed by Christ. A person whose mind is polluted and whose vision is not clear cannot understand or interpret behavior based on obedience to God.

So if you're living a different value system than the world around you, EXPECT criticism.

It just goes with being a person of faith in a culture that either doesn't understand or value faith.

Today, make your vision clear and don't apologize for your values.

Take notice of what others are saying.

Mrs. Jones invited a world famous violinist to perform at her afternoon tea. When it was over, everyone crowded around the musician. One guest said, "To be honest, I thought your performance was terrible!"

Hearing this, Mrs. Jones said to the musician, "Don't pay any attention to him. He only repeats what he hears everyone else say."

There are times you and I really need to listen to criticism, especially when there's a consensus that we are doing a bad job leading.

If reliable people on your board, in your membership, or your co-workers are saying the same critical things about you...and to you, then it's time to take inventory and start to change.

Take inventory of your criticisms today.

Rise Above Negative People

When you have optional time, spend it with people who will build you up, not with people who will tear you down.

Enough quality time with positive people will minimize the effect of negative criticism. It will also discourage you from being critical.

When a hawk is attacked by crows, he doesn't counter-attack. Instead, he soars higher and higher until the pests leave him alone.

Rise above negative people.

If your positive approach to life and faith in God has an effect on negative people, it will be because of your example, not your defensiveness.

So, rise above them. Be an eagle and don't let the turkeys get you down.

Abraham Lincoln is the most beloved of U.S. Presidents.

He was also the most criticized.

Probably no politician in history had worse things said about him. When he gave the Gettysburg Address in 1865, the Chicago Times reviewed it as "silly, flat and dishwatery utterances."

Time has proven that review to be dead wrong.

Time is your best ally; it allows you to prove yourself right. As events unfold, the cause for criticism is eliminated and you will be vindicated.

So, hang in there. If you know your action or decision was right, time is on your side, and time will prove you out.

We've all heard the slogan, "It doesn't matter whether you win or lose...until you've lost!"

Winning increases our self-image, our outlook on life and lifts our expectation level. It gives us confidence that we can succeed again.

As Christ followers, it's very simple. Every day we can walk in victory, even when it looks like defeat.

When we walk in victory and experience a growing number of wins along the way, it too gives us the hope and encouragement to continue on in this life of faith, knowing that God's in charge and loves us—and that he has it all under control!

Let today be a day that you walk in victory in and through Jesus Christ.

Are you an encourager? If so, great! If not, become one!

The KEY to encouragement is in knowing what gives people courage, what spurs them on to action.

Too many of us take pleasure in discouraging people by pointing out their mistakes and getting excited about their failures rather than their potential. What kind of self-destructive behavior is that?

Hey, encourage people. Reward them for right behavior and for getting the right results. Don't let your biggest contribution of the day be that of tearing someone down. Use your skills to inspire others to excellence.

Remember leader, people are encouraged to continue that behavior which brings them rewards...and affirmation!

Encourage and Reward

As you lead today, encourage and reward quality work instead of fast work that's mediocre.

Consider this skeletal anatomy of an organization: The wishbones wish somebody else would do the work. The jawbones talk a lot, but do little else. The knucklebones knock what everyone else does. And the backbones... they actually do the work!

Don't let this be the process of your organization!

Encourage and reward quality work! The product you produce needs to be something that the organization can be proud of and that reflects the quality of your passion for excellence.

There are great payoffs for backbone work!

Thank God today for those in your life who can figure out how to do things better and cheaper while not sacrificing quality and excellence.

Everyone, if honest, struggles with fears in life.

When it comes down to you and fear, you have three choices: You can avoid it. You can hope it goes away. Or, you can face it. And good leaders face their fears. That's not easy... but at the end of the day, that's the only thing that works.

A university study concluded that:

60% of our fears are totally unwarranted... they never come to pass.

20% of our fears are totally out of our control.

4% of our fears could be considered justifiable.

Hey, my leader/friend, let's start today by giving our fears to God. Take having faith in Him–and His control over our lives, to a whole new level.

Courageous Coward

The best leaders know themselves well.

General George Patton is considered to be one of the most bold, courageous leaders in military history. But Patton was tempted often with fear.

He said, "I am not a brave man. The truth is I am a coward at heart. In battle, I constantly have sweat on my palms and a lump in my throat."

But Patton learned how to face his fears. When he made an important decision for battle, he listened to every fear he had and weighed them against all the facts. Then, he decided to act. At that point, he turned off his fears and went ahead.

If you're making a big decision today and your palms are sweating, write down your fears, lay out the facts; ask God for wisdom—then turn off your fears and decide.

Some of the most effective leaders in the world learned a long time ago that they could reproduce themselves by taking emerging leaders on the journey with them.

But, raising people around you to a higher level involves more than just giving them information or skill. Effective leaders know they need to also empower those around them with encouragement.

Develop your skills in making other people feel important.

The Apostle Paul did this in book after book in the Bible. When a person doesn't feel good about themselves, it doesn't matter how many resources or opportunities you give them. You see, they never believe they can be successful.

But when a person senses their proper worth and value in God's eyes and yours, they will be ripe for success.

How will you encourage others today?

Give a man a fish and he eats for a day. Teach a man to fish and he eats for a lifetime..

If you want to help people, just don't give them a fish, instead give them a fishing rod and some bait. You and I can't grow another person, but we can give him/her the equipment and a process to develop them.

Around the world, EQUIP is training Christian leaders to be better Christian leaders. In over 100 nations, EQUIP is giving over three million leaders fish and fishing poles in the form of resources, training and encouragement over three - year intervals of intentional personal growth and development. These leaders are leading churches, running businesses and trying to bring transformation to their countries.

Teach a man to fish... and he eats for a lifetime.

How are you developing those around you - empowering and equipping them in leadership?

I recently read that 87% of all people fail, not because of capability but because of personality. Wow!

People usually don't fall because they can't do the job, it's because they can't get along with their co-workers. If you work just for yourself, you may not need too many relational skills. But if you work with people, you need to have or develop the ability to interact with them positively. You need to be able to simply talk to people. And, it's important to listen to people too.

Now before you stop reading, I want to challenge you to start working on your people skills. You can do this.

The fact is—you must work on your people skills if you want to experience greater success.

Begin today!

King David was a man after God's own heart. But David never hesitated to reveal his emotions or his weaknesses.

Even as King of Israel, he declared his fears, his anxieties, and his ambitions. And in the Psalms, he prayed to God about his needs for guidance, his need to handle stress, and his need to be delivered from his enemies.

Good leaders know how to balance transparency with being an example. Good leaders feel secure enough to be vulnerable. With whom are you secure enough to be vulnerable?

Is there anyone in your life who you can turn to who helps you process your need for guidance or to face the stress you're under right now?

It's a good idea to go to the Lord first.

But it's also a good idea to go to a person or persons to help you bear your burdens of leadership?

Be honest, be transparent.

The Ultimate Shepherd

No Psalm has gained more admirers than Psalm 23.

In it, we learn not only about God's nature, but also about His leadership.

David describes the Lord as a shepherd, no doubt seeing Him this way because of his own leadership bias. David also had been a model shepherd.

Both the Old and New Testaments use the word "shepherd" to illustrate leadership. The word communicates the love, nurture, intimacy and spiritual care a godly leader provides. It involves the rod of correction and the staff of direction.

Psalm 23 describes the ultimate shepherd... the Lord God.

Today, thank God that He's your shepherd giving correction and direction to your life.

You Can't Separate Leadership
from Relationships

Many leaders commit the error of separating leadership from relationships.

This happens when a person steps into a leadership position and assumes that everyone will follow his or her ideas because of his or her position.

Some leaders wrongly believe that their knowledge alone qualifies them to lead others. People don't care how much you know until they know how much you care.

We cannot separate leadership from relationships. Leaders help themselves by developing good relational skills.

How are you doing when it comes to leading others through relationships? Remember, it's an error in judgment to separate leadership from relationships.

OCT
DAY 05

To God be the Glory

It's natural for leaders to want a bit of glory or credit.

Most leaders enjoy the spotlight and feel it's only human to want their ego stroked from time to time.

However, the Apostle Paul resisted this tendency to pursue the glory that only God deserves. He focused on the superiority of God and throughout his writings teaches leaders some valuable truths about who should get all the glory and all the credit. Paul knew that human leaders must respond in humility, must seek dependence on God and not seek to get the glory that only God deserves.

The next time you and I want some of the spotlight, let's remember it's the Light of the World that gets all the glory, praise and dominion!

Love should be the foundation for every act of a leader.

In the early church, leaders modeled love to their people. In turn, the churches modeled it to the rest of the world.

They lived by the words of 1 Corinthians 13–love was the foundation and the motive for their actions. They loved their people by serving them.

Authentic love is sacrificial, others-focused love. It cares more about the needs of others than the needs of one's self.

Love makes burdens lighter because you share them and challenges easier because you divide them into manageable tasks.

Paul loved the people he led...and the world has never been the same since.

Every leader needs to love the people they're leading, especially you!

Sometimes godly leaders have to humble themselves and seek reconciliation with those they lead–even when they have done nothing wrong.

In 1 Corinthians, Paul wrote about some teachers in the church at Corinth who were abusing his teaching. As a result, he had to confront them. But the nature of his confrontation was loving in tone and his words reflected a broken heart over their actions. Paul found no joy in correcting them, but he had to clear the air and set the record straight.

Such is the price of leadership.

Today, if you're facing a situation where you have to correct some things, do it with a spirit of love and humility. It really is the best approach. You'll find that it will motivate and not humiliate.

A leader must have self-discipline.

In the Old Testament, Job finds himself with all hell breaking loose. The man lost almost everything: his livestock, his land, his home and even his children.

However, Job had self-discipline. He lived his life from his character, not his emotions or circumstances.

And after every kind of tragedy had hit him he "fell to the ground and worshipped God." What discipline!

Job never held a grudge against God and throughout the hellish ordeal of his life he maintained a sense of peace and integrity.

Job reminds every leader that self-discipline gets one through the trials–and self-discipline comes from knowing the very heart and purpose of God.

Whatever trials you face in your daily life, how about worshipping God through them? Then you will find His peace in every circumstance.

Leaders can stand strong in the face of scrutiny.

All of Job's friends posed a theory about his troubles, but Job simply asked them to survey his life and point out any place where he lacked integrity. He felt so certain of the blamelessness of his heart that he invited the scrutiny of his peers.

That's something only a secure leader will do.

C.S. Lewis called this quality, "leaders with chest."

Lewis likened the properly ordered soul to the human body. He said the "chest" was life character and spirit. Without a strong chest, men succumb to no character, hence, no chest.

Job's chest of character is a great symbol to you to be strong and to have courage.

"Though He slay me, yet I trust Him."

This kind of statement confounds a lot of people, yet it is exactly the kind of affirmation that God uses to build His Kingdom, even in the darkest places on the planet.

Here's the statement again: "Though He slay me, yet I trust Him."

That statement shook the very gates of hell.

What can stop a leader who has made that kind of commitment because he has gotten to know that kind of God? Pain and death can't. Hardship and loss can't.

You see Job was willing to put his life on the line for God.

It's only then that we today can, like Job back then, experience true liberation as a leader.

God encourages us to fix our eyes on the things that endure.

In light of eternity, leaders cannot become consumed with the temporary. Leaders can't allow the pursuit of wealth or power to move them.

Only a vision that outlives them, a vision connected to eternity, will fulfill a godly leader. In other words, we need to build a legacy. What are we going to leave behind when we die? We take nothing with us after death—no matter how rich we become.

So what will we leave behind that counts? How about doing something that lives on long after you're gone?

It's not about leaving something *to* those who follow, but about leaving something *in* those who follow.

What will your legacy be?

King David's leadership succeeded through a two-sided coin: his hands AND his heart.

He had outward skill and inward integrity. Every great spiritual leader must have this combination.

David's excellent leadership combined both heart and hands. To have one without the other, leads to failure.

Psalm 78:72 sums David up this way, "He shepherded them according to the integrity of his heart and guided them by the skillfulness of his hands."

David focused on both the spiritual formation and the skill foundation in leadership. David kept growing in his leadership with God and with men.

Together, they made him Israel's greatest king.

Are you using both your hands and heart to lead?

Modeling/Management/Memories

God calls parents to lead their children. He tells them to "train up their child/children in the way they should go."

Becoming a good leader for your children can be summed up with three key words:

Modeling: A good example is worth a thousand lectures. What you do has more impact than what you say.

Management: We are to train a child in the way he or she should go. This means we have to adapt our style depending on the temperament or the wiring of our children.

Memories: Parents should create memories... and here's why–memories are more important than things.

Modeling, Management, Memories. Great planning.

How are you planning to lead your children or those around you?

Preparation + God's Providence = Success

Leaders and organizations constantly make plans.

This is one reason why leaders are in demand; they plan and negotiate the future.

Yet back in the Old Testament, Isaiah issues a warning to every leader who develops plans without asking if they fit into the will of God.

Leaders must remember just how tentative strategic plans need to be.

No one knows the future except God. So keep in mind the following equation as you plan: Our preparation plus God's providence equals success.

As a leader, you must constantly ask if your plans fit into God's plan for you and your organization.

Sacrifice Without Question

Jesus Christ gave up the riches of heaven in order to fulfill His divinely ordained role on earth.

Isaiah describes what is often called the exchanged life...Jesus took our sin, pain and failures so we could have His righteousness, forgiveness and victory.

Servant leaders should sacrifice without question, if only for the reason that it's what Jesus would want leaders to do.

Imagine an office environment where employees knew their leader was a servant. Imagine the impact of their lives and their work.

What Jesus did on the cross can have a major impact on what we do in the office.

Have Jesus on your mind today at work and live out His sacrificial example!

The Power of Fasting

The practice of fasting goes much deeper than going without food.

God declares that fasting has power to loose the bonds of wickedness and to release heavy burdens for the oppressed.

Leaders do well to learn from these words. God is calling us to live from His set of values and ethics.

Fasting is good—and we should do it more—but to fast and still hold ungodly thoughts toward others does not reflect Godly leadership.

Ethics supply the foundation for our values. And values supply the power that drives our leadership.

Leader, consider fasting. And while fasting, consider forgiveness.

The prophet Jeremiah illustrates the leader's job as a watchman.

God appointed watchmen over His people to sound the trumpet in times of danger and to serve as His voice.

A watchman provides an outstanding metaphor for a leader.

Watchmen guard and guide those they supervise. They guard against anything that would endanger the vision. Watchmen must possess strong moral fiber and must remain committed to the strong sense of right and wrong.

In your own leadership, where do you draw the line between doing what is right and doing what will make you more popular among your followers?

What is your ultimate priority?

What should you pursue more than anything else? Wealth? Investments? Intelligence, strategy, strength, speed?

The prophet Jeremiah warns us against boasting about all of these. These are valuable resources, but not ultimate priorities.

The only thing worth boasting about is a vital relationship with God.

The others are merely a means to an end. And leaders must recognize the difference between these two.

Here's what we know from Jeremiah: God is the source, He provides life and spiritual things aren't just a means, they are the end.

Make God your priority every day.

Leaders must stand by their God-given vision!

The prophet Daniel, like any godly leader, craved insight from the Lord. But Daniel wanted more than to receive a vision from God; he wanted God to explain the vision. The Lord obliged, but also showed Daniel the price attached to such a privilege.

Do you *realize* the cost of receiving a genuine vision from God? After Daniel got his vision, he fainted and was sick in bed for days!

The point? It's just no trivial matter to receive a genuine word from God.

So if you're asking God for a vision for the future, be prepared for the enormity of the task and the responsibility you'll have to fulfill that vision!

God calls leaders to live on a higher level than followers. And one of the things leaders must keep before them is justice.

When leaders act unjustly, their influence creates a ripple effect.

God hates injustice, but especially among leaders whose crooked influence infects an entire nation!

Leadership abuses include abandoning morality, confusing values, taxing the poor for selfish gain, bribery and overall corruption.

The scary part of all this is when leaders can't see their own corruption.

If you are a part of this kind of corrupt company or even worse, one of the primary leaders of such an unjust organization, *wake up.*

There is a dreadful day of judgment coming.

And, you need to *repent.*

God is truly the ultimate leader who governs the affairs of mankind.

Who can fully grasp God's method of dealing with the world around us?

The Old Testament prophet Habakkuk, shows how God influences nations to perform His will.

Sometimes God exerts a restraining influence, and other times, God exerts a softening influence. And sometimes God exerts a directing influence. Through restraint, God prevents people from doing what they are naturally inclined to do.

Through directing He causes good to result from the evil that others intend.

Whatever the method, remember this: God is involved in global affairs and will get all glory for what happens on this planet.

Leadership means you lose your right to be selfish.

The builders in the prophet Haggai's day had left their original purpose to construct the temple and instead went to work on their own houses and businesses.

It took a leader like Haggai to call them back to their primary purpose. When leaders and people fail to maintain proper priorities, disappointment always results.

Remember, 20% of your effort will get 80% of the desired results. But with the wrong priorities, 80% of your effort will get you 20% of the desired results.

It's not about working harder, but smarter. Knowing and living out your priorities really matters!

Good leaders are continual learners. We must keep learning or we'll stop leading.

We can't afford to stagnate, because our world and our people are changing just too quickly. New insights and new opportunities, appear all the time.

Good leaders have lots of ways to keep learning... including learning lessons from the past. Looking back at when our forefathers obeyed God, or disobeyed God, that's a great idea.

If we don't learn from the past—as the saying goes—we're destined to repeat it.

So why not grab some binoculars and take a closer took at what happened in the past? And from that lesson, lead today and tomorrow.

OCT
DAY 24
Fruits of the Spirit

The fruits of the Spirit in Galatians 5 are not only to be seen in good times, but in tough times too.

These Christian graces of love, joy, peace, patience, goodness, kindness–and all the others–should be graces flowing especially from leaders.

Every one of these attributes is given so that they will become part of a DAILY life; and in *evidence* for all to see when things go wrong. So, if someone is really hungry and becomes irritable toward you, give him a piece of bread with butter. That's showing kindness! But when you throw some jam on it, that's leading with kindness.

As a leader, even in your kindness, your joy, your peace and your love - do a little more and a little better than everyone else.

How do you react when you're criticized?

There's always someone out there who is going to criticize you, especially if you're a leader. Some are so good at being critical, you wonder if they're being paid for it. The numbers are mammoth when it comes to the people who have been hurt "under the banner" of constructive criticism.

Here's an interesting observation: It is constructive criticism when I criticize you; it's destructive criticism when you criticize me!

Now, whether criticism is just or unjust, the real test is how we respond when criticism comes our way. The best way to lose an enemy is to treat them like a friend.

Just as your Heavenly Father gives you mercy when you need justice, that's the model for you when you're tempted to be critical of those being critical of you.

Have Mercy!

Is it Biblical to lead?

Christians have debated the subject of leadership for years.

Are we not called to be followers instead of leaders? Are we not called to be servants instead of rulers?

Well, consider this...the first description of mankind in the Bible involves leadership. And God said after He made man that it would be man's job to "rule" and have authority over all the earth.

If God told us to rule, that means we must have the ability to rule.

Think about it: Today, you have the ability to lead someone else in some area of life!

Shoulder to Shoulder

As a leader of your family and as a member of the body of Christ, you are standing shoulder to shoulder with others in the work of God. You are not working alone.

God has made each one of us to work differently, but also to work together. You have a place to fill, a role to play that no else can. Without a doubt, you will encounter opposition. Your personal circumstances may seem to conspire against your successful completion of the task before you. You may be criticized by others who don't like how you're doing your part. You may even begin to question the worth of what you're going to do.

But remember this leader: you are never alone.

First pray. Set your defenses against the opposition and keep going. Fulfill your role with confidence in God and persist in doing good. Don't let your part remain undone.

The work of God is to be done by the people of God according to the will of God.

Drop Your Excuses and Lead

Leaders don't allow excuses to stand in the way of reaching their full potential.

Do you remember reading about Moses at the burning bush? When he faced that bush in Exodus 3, he felt inadequate and unprepared to lead. But that's what God called him to do. Many potential leaders in the Bible were afraid and ran from their call.

Most of us can list why we don't lead effectively, just as Moses did. When God called on him to lead he used excuse after excuse.

Now, what's your excuse? Too shy? Too scared? Too stubborn?

Today, drop your excuses to lead; respond to God's call to lead in your family, your neighborhood, your church, or your business.

The most effective leaders perceive a great need.

In Judges, there were no leadership positions to fill. There was no protocol or structure at all. There was no voting. If you led, it was because you saw a need and got other people to help you. A lot of the judges in the book of Judges got their start when they saw a specific problem they could address.

Pure leadership starts with a need and sparks a passion. Then, others respond to the need and move others to get involved.

Remember, the most effective leaders perceive a great need.

See any needs around you today?

When an outward need in your community or church matches up with an inward gifting in your life, as a leader, you will be consumed with passion to meet that need.

The passion becomes apparent to others–and then others want to get involved.

In the book of Judges, several leaders had a kind of inward chemistry that sparked an outer passion. Passion is amazing. It makes up for a lack of resources. Resources are great, but the Judges of the Bible weren't flush with lots of cash or options.

But what they did have–and it defined their leadership–was passion!

What is your inward gifting? What are you passionate about? Now do something about it!

OCT DAY 31

Rise Up

In every age, there comes a time when a leader must come forward to meet the needs of the hour.

Therefore, there is no potential leader who does not have the opportunity to make a positive difference in society. Tragically, there are times when a leader does not rise to that hour.

Why is it that when circumstances call for it, a leader does not rise to that hour? Many times, it's because that leader has not prepared his or her heart to serve. A mission that is critical to our success in leadership is having a "servant heart."

When we lose our heart for what God's called us to do, we lose our ability to lead others to a better way of living.

Will you rise up today and have a servant's heart?.

In John 13, Jesus modeled a servant's heart when He washed the disciples' feet.

Now, what enabled Him to do this? It was a strong sense of security. Leaders who are not secure in their identity in Christ will eventually sabotage their leadership.

Insecure leaders become their own worst enemies. They cannot share victories or sorrows. For the insecure leader, it's all about them.

Only secure leaders give their power and attention to others.

Secure leaders want to add value to others. Insecure leaders want to gain value from others.

Will you share in the example modeled by Christ and be a secure leader today?

Once a leader has clarified and shared the vision, he or she can focus on serving and being responsive to the needs of the people.

By understanding that the role of leadership is to remove barriers and help people achieve the vision, the greatest leaders can mobilize people.

This is done by gathering people around a shared vision.

A compelling vision creates a strong culture in which the energy of everyone in the organization is aligned.

What's your vision? Have you made it clear and compelling as you share it? Maybe it's time to think about better ways to share the vision with those you need to carry it out.

Mistaken priorities lie at the heart of ineffective leadership.

In Matthew 23, Jesus scolded the Pharisees for confusing what was and wasn't important. Their priorities were enforcing laws and rules. Christ's priorities were the spiritual needs of others.

Great leaders know the heart of their people and act with that end in mind. As spiritual leaders, we know that Jesus died for us and that our ultimate, priority mission is the Great Commission.

Consequently, we always need to ask God for wisdom, keeping that big picture in mind.

Do you have any mistaken priorities that need to be handed over to God?

Leaders who have it together know how to say, "No."

They do it gracefully, but they do it... they say "No." When you say no, make it clear to the person you are declining to that you're not rejecting them...just the idea. You can affirm the idea–even love the idea–but at the end of the day, if the idea doesn't fit the plan of your leadership, you have to be able to say no.

The fact is that you and I can say no much easier when we know our life purpose.

If you know who you are, what your gifts are and what your calling is, then no is a word you have to learn to say regularly and graciously.

Three Attitudes

In their good book, *Toybox Leadership*, authors Hunter and Waddell write about three attitudes that promote a confident face:

First, there is the Sense of Identity: Be secure in who you are. People can tell if you believe in yourself or don't believe in yourself.

Next, have a Sense of Purpose. Understand where and how you fit into the world around you.

And finally, have a Sense of Competence. Competence is having the skills and experience to properly carry out what is expected of you.

Today, as a child of God, make sure you demonstrate a confident face and heart!

Our U.S. coins are engraved with the motto: IN GOD WE TRUST.

These are some powerful words that reflect the values of a previous generation. But do they reflect the values of our present generation? Are we living with the conviction that "without faith, it is impossible to please God?"

Young leaders have a lot of places to center their trust. But a life of faith is the most exemplary life of all.

A life of faith challenges a leader at his/her core.

Here's a test for you if you are a young leader...as gifted as you are, can you look in the mirror, face yourself and say: "In God and God alone, I trust?"

Your answer is going to tell you a lot.

The best leaders take risks.

No one ever stubs his or her toe while standing still.

FDR once said, "It is common sense to take a method and try it. But above all, try SOMETHING." Failing to try because of a desire to be secure is going to result in a failure to lead.

Bill Hybels says it this way: "Every single day we make choices. We choose whether we are courageous or cowardly. We choose between the right thing and the convenient thing."

Today in your leadership, choose to do courageous and right things over the cowardly and convenient things. To do anything else is failure.

Where Do You Turn?

Where do you turn when you are lost?

My friend Paul Borthwick admits he's not much of an outdoors man, but he has profound respect for a friend of his who is.

Here's how Paul describes his outdoor friend Gerry. "If I were lost in the wilderness, I would want to be with Gerry. He is not the strongest or most athletic hiker I've ever met, but he knows the forest–and in the challenge of being lost, he would know how to keep us alive."

That's really what the best leaders do. In the midst of times when things get confused, even lost, leaders know where to turn and where to find the resources needed to make it through the toughest challenges.

Where do you turn in a challenge?

Every leader need not be brilliant; but leaders should be knowledgeable.

Jesus commands that we follow Him and learn from Him. Christian leaders need knowledge of the Bible. But they also need knowledge of themselves. And, it helps to have knowledge of people too.

Finally, leaders should have knowledge of our world because our world is rapid and complex–ever changing.

And in this ever-changing world, we need leaders who can fully tap the knowledge available to them so that they can effectively lead the Church in bringing the gospel to the world.

Will you be this kind of knowledgeable leader?

Give Respect Freely but Expect to Earn it From Others

A leader needs to give respect freely but also expect to earn it from others.

One day a man was arriving at the airport and saw a well-dressed businessman yelling at a porter about the way he was handling his luggage.

The more irate the businessman became the calmer and more professional the porter appeared. When the abusive man left, the first man complimented the porter on his restraint.

"Oh, it was nothing," said the porter. "You know, that man's going to Miami, but his bags–they're headed for Kalamazoo."

People who disrespect others always hurt themselves relationally–and they often react in negative ways.

Here's what we know, to be a great leader you need to treat people with respect. That just goes along with the leadership responsibility.

The best way to start off on the right foot is to put others first.

The most basic way to do that is to practice the Golden Rule: "Do unto others as you would have them do unto you."

If you take that mindset into all of your interactions with others, you just can't go wrong. But there are other ways as well to show people that they matter: you can walk slowly by them, say considerate things toward them, remember their names, smile at people and be quick to offer help.

People don't care how much you know until they know how much you care.

How are you showing that you care?

**Give Time to Your Most
Valuable Relationships**

A leader plans to give the most time to the most valuable people in their lives.

Most people give away their relational energy on a first-come, first-serve basis. Whoever gets their attention first gobbles up their time and relational energy.

That's why the squeaky wheels instead of high producers at work consume so much attention and why so many people have nothing left to give when they get home from work.

Family provides that most valuable relationship of your life. Family should come first.

Spend time with your family today.

Giving Turns Your Focus Outward

Here's what a literary critic once wrote,

"How delightful is the company of generous people, who overlook trifles and keep their minds instinctively fixed on whatever is good and positive in the world around them.

Now compare that to people who are small of caliber; they are people who are always showing their superiority, their knowledge, their prowess or their good breeding.

But magnanimous people have no vanity, no jealousy, no reserves, and they feed on what is true and solid wherever they find it."

How great it is to be around magnanimous people.

Giving Adds Value to Others

To be a good leader, you must add value to others.

U.S. President Woodrow Wilson said it this way: "You are not here merely to make a living. You are here in order to enable the world to live more amply, with greater vision, with a finer spirit of home and achievement. You are here to enrich the world and you impoverish yourself if you forget the errand."

No one stands taller in the climb to success than the person who is willing to bend over to help up someone else.

As a leader, add value to others, and when you do that you don't take anything away from yourself.

Everyone you meet is fighting a hard battle. The other person's life is no easier than yours.

Perhaps today he or she is only misunderstood and hurt. A sure indication that a person hurts inside is the confirmation of what he or she says on the outside.

Out of a person's heart flow words that either win or wound. Such a person may hurt you by what he or she says or does because of that inward hurt.

When a hurting person tries to hurt you, a reaction of kind and positive words and mannerisms can go a long way in communicating the kind of Christian graces taught in Galatians 5...graces like love, joy, peace and kindness.

Today leader, will you offer up words that will win or wound others?

Every leader is busy these days. There are schedules to follow, goals to achieve, problems to solve, appointments to keep, jobs to finish and deadlines to meet.

If you're weary on the journey, let me encourage you to stop, get quiet and get some rest.

It's time to turn off some of the noise!

In Romans 12, we are reminded that the world around us can squeeze us into its own mold. It's very easy, in our desire to "get 'r done" to let the pressures of the crowd or our peers start us off in the wrong direction. It's easy to follow the lines of least resistance.

And as a leader, you need to remember that when you are tempted to cut corners and negate discipline, it's time to stop and reevaluate your life.

History is a great teacher! Experience is a hard worker!

Only by taking time to reflect on yesterday and honestly evaluate its successes and failures can we learn and prepare for tomorrow.

Your willingness to learn and adjust positively from yesterday's mistakes and short-comings are mission-crucial in determining just how far you will travel down the road to success.

While we need to leave what is behind, it's always wise or street smart to learn from what we left behind.

After all, those are the lessons, the failures and the successes–the history of our lives that have brought us to this very moment.

History is a great teacher–if you'll just pay attention in class!

Every leader in any kind of relationship, is tempted to quit.

Ralph Waldo Emerson said, "A man is a hero not because he is braver than anyone else, but because he is braver for ten minutes longer."

Every track runner knows that to run long distances you need to get your second wind. He runs until he's just about out of gas and full of pain—but if he waits just a little longer and runs a little further, he'll get his second wind.

Until a person has tried hard enough and long enough to get his second wind, he'll never know how much he can accomplish.

If you're tempted to quit, about out of gas and full of pain, ask God to help you take a few more steps.

Before you know it, you'll get your second wind.

There's no better way to change a problem than to help someone see a solution.

Many times people with problems become slaves to their situation because they can see nothing but problems.

The saying, "I can't see the forest through the trees," is applicable here.

The best leaders help others see the potential in all their situations.

Many times people will tell me, "I'm sure you've never had to deal with a problem like mine." They feel their problem is unique. They are filled with self-pity.

Part of your role as a leader is to help others get out of their dungeon and into the activity of helping them solve their problem... focusing on the positive solutions and answers.

A newspaper reporter went to visit an old man upon the celebration of his 100th birthday. The reporter approached him and asked, "Sir, you must have seen a great many changes during your one hundred years."

The old man gazed at him and said, "Yes, and I've been against every one of them."

You know— if we're not careful, we can get stuck in a rut and let the world pass us by after we've raised all of our objections to all the changes.

What's sad for those who resist change is this–few things can improve, few people can improve...except through change!

But change for the sake of change isn't the goal. Remember, change for the sake of true growth is one of life's most noble goals.

Anyone who walks down the path of life not only has the privilege of enjoying it, but also must take the risk of falling.

When you rise to the occasion, you may fall prey to the enemy. Any person who is willing to stand for something all the time will be knocked down.

Leaders, especially leaders in the Kingdom of God, should stand for something–and for Someone, the Lord Jesus.

But even when we make that stand, sometimes we fumble our words, lose our thoughts, say the wrong things, embarrass our family members, and even disappoint our Lord.

But that's part of the growth plan for leaders. When we fall, we learn humility and grace.

And in that lesson, you'll learn how to walk better–and lead better for the future.

There's lots of success in the marketplace today. Perhaps the best definition of success I've seen is: "Success is losing a life and finding it."

Jesus said, "Whoever finds his life will lose it, and whoever loses his life for my sake will find it."

What you keep, you lose, and what you lose you keep. Quite a paradox!

One of the reasons many have never tasted sweet success is that they're unwilling to sacrifice to achieve.

Life is usually a just bargainer.

You give a little, and you receive a little. You give much, and you receive much. Every leader needs to remember that losing is winning in God's eyes!

If that thought scares you, maybe you need a new set of glasses.

Have you ever met anyone who believes that success comes from taking advantage of opportunities?

There is some truth in that, but it's rather one-dimensional. The problem with folks believing success is just taking advantage of opportunities is that they often spend a great deal of their time regretting "lost" opportunities.

These are the "if only" folks. "If only my boss would give me a chance; If only my wife would...if only my church would..."

You get the idea. Look, if all we do is wait for opportunity to come our way, we won't be ready when it comes.

Listen, if your ship came in tomorrow morning, what in the world would you do with it? You don't even have a harbor to anchor it.

So get busy today planning for tomorrow's opportunities. Don't wait!

We should be thankful to God because HE is our maker and provider. All that we are and all that we have is from God's hand.

Food to consume. Air to breathe. Time to live. Blood flowing through our veins. Shelter. Friendships.

We ought to be thankful.

For grief that we didn't suffer. For the clouds that scattered and the dangers that passed us by.

Life comes from God.

And every necessity of life comes from God.

The Psalmist said it better than I ever could. "Know that the Lord, He is God. It is He who made us, and not we ourselves."

Remember this today and be thankful - God is your provider.

There's always something to thank God for!

One comic said, "If you can't pay your bills, be thankful you're not one of your creditors!"

Another comic said, "I don't realize how much I have to be thankful for until I have to start paying taxes for it."

Okay, enough of the stand-up comedy.

Here's what we know: We should be thankful to God. He is our Maker and Provider. He is worthy to receive glory, honor and power.

It's no joke that God is worthy of our thanks–this Thanksgiving and every Thanksgiving to follow.

Be thankful my friend!

God is good all the time–and all the time, God is good.

In every circumstance and every situation, the Bible teaches us that we are to give thanks. It's my belief that a child of God has the capacity to give thanks like no other.

It's a unique capacity that children of God have—to thank God—for everything and everybody.

We know that God never allows anything unplanned. God is never taken by surprise.

And God always makes all things work together for good.

Unbelievers may scoff and scorn, but Christ followers know deep in their hearts that God is taking even the things that seem impossible to give thanks for, and turning them into opportunities to give Him even greater thanks.

Give thanks always for the many things God gives you.

All things work together for good!

That's what the Bible says in Romans 8:28. There is completeness with that statement... ALL things.

Somehow, in the economy of God this Thanksgiving, you and I have the capacity to give thanks in the midst of loss, tragedy and heartache.

Is it possible to give thanks, for everything?

God's word says that it is. All things, everything!

In the delightful things, the difficult things, even the devilish things, we can give thanks.

A life of un-thankfulness carries with it a high price. It rejects the rightful place of a sovereign God in our lives.

So today, give thanks—because all the circumstances of your life as a Christ follower are in His hands.

While we reflect on the knowledge that all things work together for good, why are people still discontented, especially at work?

Why do we sometimes want to just quit?

EQUIP's founder, John C. Maxwell says that there are usually 1 of 4 reasons people will quit organizations when they're uneasy about staying around: 1. When they feel devalued by their employer, 2. When they find their employer untrustworthy, 3. When they find their employer incompetent, 4. When they find their employer insecure.

People want to work for people who fire them up–not people who put out their fire! People want mentors who lift them, not try to hold them down.

Here's the truth: If people perceive that their leader is more concerned with their authority and protecting their position, they will eventually find somebody else to work for and you can bank on that.

Today, put some thought towards how you can feed the fire of those around you.

Leaders sometimes have to make wrong decisions in order to learn how to make the right ones!

Ted Engstrom used to tell the story about the governing board of a bank who chose a bright young man to succeed their retiring president. The young man set up a meeting with the old man. "Sir, what is the main thing I must possess to successfully follow you as the president of this bank?"

The old man replied: "The ability to make decisions."

"How do I learn to do that?" asked the young banker.

"Experience," the older banker said.

"And how do I get experience?" asked the young banker.

The old man said, "Bad decisions."

Every bad decision we've made should help us to be better leaders!

So, let's learn from bad decisions. Since we have experience that has cost us so very much, let's not make such "costly" decisions in the future.

A Meeting BEFORE the Meeting

Do you just LOVE meetings? Or, do you just hate them?

Most leaders find meetings to be a burden–but they've also learned that if they're going to take people on the journey with them, there are times when you have to sit down and meet. So, it seems that if we need to have meetings, we should really try to make them better than average–actually try to make them productive.

So, if you are going to be running a meeting in the future, here's a thought in helping you make it more productive: Have a meeting BEFORE the meeting!

Spend time on the phone or in person with some key people you need (as related to certain issues), and gain their perspective and support before the "big" meeting ever takes place. You'll find the pre-meeting will go a long way toward making the big meeting smoother and more efficient.

Do you have a meeting coming up that you're responsible for? Why not have a meeting before that meeting?

It's a bit mystifying, but people who make it a regular practice to reflect on their past experiences, well, they are just rare to find.

But when you meet that rare person, it doesn't take you long to know it. The school of life offers many difficult courses. Some of them we sign up for willingly. Others, we're just surprised that we've even enrolled.

But here's the deal... every experience of life can teach us some valuable lessons. But those experiences are only valuable if we take the time to reflect–and truly desire to learn from them. The Bible teaches that wisdom comes from God–who wants to take us forward–but also wants us to remember what we've learned on the journey.

Hey, while we're so on the go, let's take time to stop and think about where we've been.

Today Matters, Part 1

People create success in their lives when they focus on today. That may sound trite, but today is the only time you have.

It's too late for yesterday. Yesterday ended last night.

It's too soon for tomorrow–tomorrow isn't guaranteed... you just don't know what tomorrow holds. That's why today matters.

In the Bible, James says we don't even know what will happen tomorrow. So, it seems wise to focus on today. The way you invest your time *today* directly affects your future.

If you take a faulty approach to today with a faulty view of success, you won't capitalize on today's potential.

"TODAY is the day the Lord has made. Rejoice, be glad"... and make the most of it. Today's decisions impact tomorrow!

The fact is we exaggerate YESTERDAY.

Were the good ole' days really that good? I don't think so.

And while we exaggerate yesterday, we overestimate tomorrow.

Like Scarlett O'Hara, we tell ourselves we'll get it all done tomorrow—exaggerating the reality of all we can get done in a day.

The truth is we underestimate today!

We tend to want to look backward or forward at yesterday or tomorrow—and forget about all we can get done TODAY.

You see, today matters!

What you do today—the work, the relationships, the decisions or the lack thereof, will all impact tomorrow.

So don't get lost in the dreams of tomorrow and forget today. Get busy making today the most important of your life!

Today Matters, Part 3

Some people get disillusioned because they feel life should be easier than it is. But life isn't easy—and to embrace the contrary is to make a faulty assumption.

The moment success doesn't come quickly, many become negative and say "I didn't want it anyway," or "I knew I couldn't achieve it from the beginning."

Why is it that some believe success is impossible? Success is possible with everyone!

If today, you would simply add value to one other person, you are a success.

Add value long enough to enough people through the years and you will have the reputation of being successful.

The most successful people in life use every day to make other people's lives successful! It's really simple.

Don't make success a disillusionment. It's attainable. And it's attainable today!

Sometimes people approach success as if it were a magic formula!

I'm not kidding. They think that all they have to do is discover the formula and magically they'll appear at the desired destination. To them, success is a mystery that requires a hunt.

All these folks don't realize that success comes through hard work and developing one's God-given gifts and talents.

One doesn't wave a magic wand or gather 4-leaf clovers to achieve success.

Both Christians and non-Christians experience success when they focus on their futures by maximizing today—that's this very day!

So, what are you focusing on? Magic? Luck? Tomorrow?

How about making TODAY matter?

The secret of your success and mine is determined by our daily agenda.

In the Bible, Daniel began living his values as a young man. And then, he lived out those values through his daily agenda. He prayed three times every day. He practiced a strict diet and knew where to draw the line on the political and social issues of his day.

He knew who he was and what he stood for–and had known those things about himself since he was a young man.

Every day, you have to manage a daily agenda.

Is your agenda and decision making a reflection of the values you embrace?

That's a good question for you if you are a person who wants to make a difference in our world.

Make Great Daily Decisions

Leaders need to be able to make great daily decisions.

When you look at the prophet Daniel in the Bible, you discover that he didn't wait to become famous in order to begin practicing important daily decisions.

In fact, it could be argued that because he first practiced good daily decisions, that over time, God entrusted Daniel with more. Daniel was preparing for his future when *no one* was watching.

His spiritual life was in great shape first, and when the time came to help the king interpret his dream and provide some wisdom and application, Daniel was right there... ready to go.

No bells, no whistles, no press releases–just a servant prepared to serve God.

Remember, there is great value in making great daily decisions... emphasis on the DAILY!

Three of the most difficult areas of life to master are these: attitude, time and health.

How do we steward these precious possessions?

As leaders, we feel it is noble to spend our lives for the sake of others. And, that is noble, indeed. However, we often do it at the expense of our own well-being.

The best leaders understand the value of ruling their attitudes, calendar and physical health. Good attitudes give us *possibilities*. The right priorities give us *focus*. And good health. It gives us *strength*!

In our desire to help others, let's not lose sight of the need that as leaders, we need to steward our thoughts, our schedules and our bodies.

The attitude I have today gives me all kinds of possibilities.

It's next to impossible for leaders to succeed without a good attitude.

Now there are some exceptions, but attitude will definitely impact just how much a leader with a bad attitude will enjoy their success!

A poor attitude can diminish the fruit we bear because it is opposed to the attitude of faith. The world's best leaders are full of faith. They actually believe and take risks in their belief.

In Scripture, we see three attitudes the best leaders possess consistently: Positive Attitude, Servant Attitude and a Determined attitude.

Do any or all of these describe you?

Attitude Matters to Leadership

Your success as a leader isn't only about your gifts, talents, IQ or even your budget. More than these, your success is about your attitude.

What kind of attitude do you possess year in and year out? Your attitude matters in your leadership.

For instance, when you begin a task, your attitude matters—it actually affects its outcome.

We are told in Philippians 2, to share the same attitude that Christ had when he came to earth.

That's an attitude that was healthy, encouraging and enduring. It's also an attitude of service.

No doubt about it...a healthy attitude helps you and others when you begin to lead people and projects.

As a leader of your family you know the importance of paying your bills!

The same thing is true for giving back to the Lord! Ministries all over this nation depend on the generous gifts of the Church body! Electric bills must be paid. Buildings and equipment must be maintained for good stewardship. The salaries of faithful workers must be met. Those kinds of ongoing needs require ongoing support!

That's where consistent, regular giving is so important and what we send in each month to God's workers is just as much an act of worship as the songs we sing or the Scriptures we study in our church every week.

Giving regularly is a wonderful demonstration of God's Lordship over your resources and your gratitude to Him for consistent care of you and your family!

During this holiday season, perhaps God is asking you to trust Him with your resources and give a gift of gratitude to His many ministries throughout the world.

Jesus placed a high value on people. Every leader should follow his example.

Romans 12:10 teaches us to be devoted to each other and outdo one another in showing honor. The New Testament actually tells us to treat others as more important than ourselves.

It's really simple—your attitude toward others often determines their attitude toward you. If you don't value people, why should they value you? If you don't value people and are in a leadership position, I predict you won't be a leader for long.

The good news is that you can decide to change your attitude about others.

If you want to continue on the leadership journey, I invite you to change your attitude. If you don't, you won't be leading, you'll be taking a walk all by yourself.

Today, focus on having a good attitude and valuing people.

I think there's real value in trying to find something positive in just about every situation.

A pastor friend of mine, when talking about a Christian's reaction to so many of the terrible things we see in the news, puts it this way: *God allows what He hates to accomplish what He loves!*

In Philippians 4, Paul wrote that he was learning to be content in every situation life handed him. For Paul, that was a secret of life.

Sadly, it's a secret not a whole lot of folks discover.

Mother Teresa was asked once what were her requirements were to work for her in the slums of Calcutta. She said simply, people who worked for her had to work hard and possess a joyful attitude–regardless of the situation.

Do you have a positive attitude?

DEC
Focus on Time
DAY 14

Given a choice, what would you rather save: Time or Money?

Most people focus on money. However, time may be more valuable than money. You can always get more money when it is lost, but you can never get more time.

Consequently, effective leaders focus on establishing priorities in order to get the most out of their time.

Paul wasn't kidding when he said, "Make the most of your time because the days are evil."

It's been said, "Devoting a little of yourself to everything means committing a great deal of yourself to nothing."

Be focused, leader, on the priorities God has placed before you!

Take Care of Yourself

Leaders often neglect the issue of HEALTH because their schedule is so busy. To spend time on our health, we rationalize, whether it is food or fitness, seems so selfish. Yeah, right.

Here's the deal: Our bodies cannot perform the tasks required of leaders if our health is out of order. The "temple" of the Holy Spirit is what God calls our bodies. Ouch, that hurts.

Reality is this: God gives us several gifts, lots of talents and plenty of opportunities. But with all that abundance, God has given us only ONE body!

So let's take care of it, leaders!

If we want to have a healthy life, here's a top ten list:

10. Handle stress well
9. Communicate well
8. Delegate well
7. Eat healthy foods as often as you can
6. Do work you enjoy
5. Accept your personal worth
4. Find your pace in life
3. Get physical exercise regularly
2. Laugh often
1. Pray well

Now, I know I'm no David Letterman and my TOP TEN LISTS could never match his.

I also know that if you want a healthy life, my TOP TEN can help you stay at the top of your leadership for a long time.

Here's a myth: Success comes from recognition.

If I just work hard to get recognized, I'll be successful.

Every profession has their own form of recognition. Some want to be recognized by their peers. Others want to be recognized outside of their peer group. Regardless, the motive to be recognized and affirmed is emotionally unhealthy and really reflects the poorest of motives.

Can I ask a hard question?

Are you in a performance trap? Are you just consumed with the idea that "if only" someone would recognize you and just how wonderful, brilliant and amazing you are, that you, Mr. or Miss Amazing Human Being, would be on the road to success?

That's all a myth.

What you need to get busy doing is just making TODAY MATTER in your life and in the lives of those around you.

There are twenty-four hours in a day and there is no way for us to change that.

There have only been two men in history for whom God allowed the "sun to stand still" so He could prolong their day. God prolonged the day for Joshua to win a battle and King Hezekiah to fulfill his dream.

Most of us don't get the luxury of approaching God and being granted a longer day. We have to make the most of the day and days we have. In fact, TODAY is really a big deal. And we need to make TODAY matter.

The Psalmist wrote, "Teach us to number our days."

That's great counsel. We have been given a mission to fulfill in our lives

and that mission begins TODAY!

Daniel was a man in the Bible who understood the importance of TODAY.

One of the greatest prophets in the Bible, Daniel could see into the future, but at his core, he cared about today. He lived during the Babylonian Captivity–one of the most difficult eras in Israel's history.

Somehow, he knew success would come early in life by making sound daily decisions. He kept that up for the rest of his life. He just kept making sound daily decisions.

It wasn't easy or glamorous, but early in his life he began some good habits. He knew that his decisions would determine his destination.

He decided well when he was young–and never regretted it.

Do you as a leader understand the importance of each and every day?

Effective people make right decisions every day and then manage those decisions in the days that follow.

Early in his life, Daniel made some fundamental decisions on some of the most strategic days of his life. Then, he spent the rest of his life managing those early decisions.

Have you made some decisions in your life about values and virtues? If you haven't, you should.

The decisions you make today about which things matter most and mean the most to you, will be with you forever. And if you manage those daily decisions early and well, it will reap great benefits to your life.

Today is a great day–in fact a wonderful day for you to make some "right" decisions. And, if you manage those decisions well in the days that follow, success is inevitable.

More than any other single factor in a person's formative years, family life forges character.

That's a big part of the reason we need strong, healthy families more than ever.

Perry Webb noted, "The home is the lens through which we get our first look at marriage, civic duties, conversations, attitudes, reverence and respect for authority."

The Apostle Paul even states that a leader whose home is out of order has a hard time leading the church. God intended for our spiritual leadership to begin in the home and then expand our leadership from there. The home is a great lab to put leadership into practice.

If your leadership doesn't work within your own family, then maybe you'd be wise not to export your leadership elsewhere.

A leader today must have courage.

Courage is the commitment to do the right thing in the face of possible criticism.

Courage is the first essential quality for effective leaders. Leaders initiate and take a stand even when no one else is traveling with them.

In the Bible, Paul encouraged Timothy to take courage and do what was right in difficult times.

Leaders have to resist the temptation that position brings of falling into pleasure's and power that ruin a leader's personal life—for the personal life is reflected in the public life.

Remember leader, courage is taking a position even when you know it might cost you everything.

Any time you are willing to stand up for something as a leader, someone else will take a shot at you.

People express their convictions and attempt to live them out and experience conflict from others with opposing views.

Ralph Waldo Emerson wrote, "Whatever you need, you need courage. Whatever course you take there is always someone to tell you that you are wrong."

"Peace has its victories" Emerson says, "but it takes bravery... it takes brave men and women to win those victories."

If the Lord Jesus Christ had his critics, it's safe to say that you will too.

The issue isn't that you will have critics, the issue is—will you be courageous when faced with criticism and not compromise your convictions?

Most of us agree that there seems to be a growing preoccupation with Christmas giving and getting. Gifts keep getting more and more elaborate and expensive.

Increasingly, it seems that the Christmas season is swallowed up by shopping, wrapping, mailing packages and cards. Christmas sales will again be at record levels–and most retailers need a strong Christmas season to put their business year in the black.

Once again, we are tempted in the busyness of the season to neglect the primary purpose of Christmas. God became flesh, dwelt among us, died a sacrificial death, so that we might receive the greatest gift of all–eternal life.

That's the real reason Christmas stands out... and my prayer is that you'll give Him praise and worship throughout the season for His amazing gift to you.

The greatest leader in history, in all eternity for that matter, came to this world in a barn in Bethlehem, was wrapped up in simple cloth and placed in a feeding trough. As beautiful as we try to make the manger scene seem, it wasn't that beautiful at all.

What was beautiful, then and now, was that God, in human form, made his way, miraculously, to this world. And the world has never been the same!

Encyclopedias devote more words and coverage to Jesus Christ than to Napoleon, Julius Caesar or Aristotle.

The true beauty of Christmas isn't in the lights, the wrappings or even the family time.

The true beauty of Christmas is that God sent to this world what we needed the most–A Savior, Christ, the Lord.

Make today all about Him.

When Jesus came to this earth as a baby, later to die on the cross, He did not die because of His own sin. Nor, did He die because he was a victim of circumstances.

He came to die as a gift to you and me.

What that means is that this Christmas season, with all the distractions around us, that we dare not MISS that great gift from Jesus.

This Christmas, Jesus still remains the only one who has died for our sins. He is the only one who can cure a broken heart and take away a rebellious spirit—and totally change a life. Jesus is a gift.

Not to be scorned or ridiculed, but that He would be worshipped and adored.

This Christmas season, don't miss the main character in the story...Jesus. He is the gift to us who brought the great gift of forgiveness.

It was no accident that the good news of Jesus' birth would be announced to an audience of shepherds. You see, God often will take the simple, the common, the average and weak in our world to fulfill His mandates.

He molded Moses on the backside of the desert. David was the youngest son from the smallest tribe in Israel–and he became King. Joseph was a slave who became Prime Minister and Jesus, when he started his public ministry, selected fishermen and tax collectors as his associates.

God takes the foolish and the simple to confound the wise.

And in Luke 2, God choose shepherds as the symbols, the reminders, of the commonness of man. We all have a common problem–sin. And, we all have a common need–forgiveness.

That's where Christ comes into the story. He is sinless and only He can forgive sin.

This Christmas, remember an uncommon Savior came to this world to redeem common folks like you and me.

Jesus was born into a world of religious chaos, social change and racial hostility. There was darkness, guilt and the fear of death.

Seneca, the Roman philosopher said, "All my life I have been trying to climb out of the pit of my sin... but I cannot and will not unless a hand is let down to lift me."

Jesus Christ is that hand that Seneca sought.

You see, because of sin, there was a great need of a costly gift. Sin so gripped the world that no one has the capacity to change themselves. We need hope. We need help.

Today, in this Christmas season, why not reach out your hand to the only one who can pull you from the pit of your sin. Today, put your hand into the hand of Jesus Christ.

When you and I reconcile our check books, our goal is to have things in balance.

This is a good reminder as we begin a new year, that if we have some relationships out there–out of balance–that we haven't tried to reconcile or restore, we're going to start the new year the way we ended the old year–out of balance!

To reconcile means to settle or resolve a dispute. It can also mean to acquiesce, to lay down a weapon. If also means to make compatible.

As this year ends, ask yourself, "Are there some people with whom I have unresolved issues?" Is there anyone with whom I need to motivate toward reconciliation with another?

These are great questions that help you to have a balanced life.

Forgive and Forget

The Apostle Paul had reason to forget what was behind. He had held the coats of those who stoned Stephen, the first Christian martyr.

We all have done things for which we are ashamed. And we live in the tension of what we have been and what we want to be.

Because of Christ, we can let go of the past guilt and look forward to what God will help us become. Don't dwell on your past.

If there are some past relationships that need mending, then start the process.

Just remember, Christ forgives and gives you the power to move forward in power and in peace.

It's a good thing to recall the past year and remember when God has been our refuge and help.

The New Year ahead and the old year past should remind us of God's goodness and challenge us to share that goodness with others. Oh, it's hats off to the old year—and move on to the New Year. There's much to be done.

Let's look ahead with hope and encouragement.

The world has a lot of problems. Paul called it a groaning planet for a reason. But if you are a Christ follower, you should see the New Year before you as the most amazing opportunity in your life.

There are dreams to pursue, mountains to climb and people to help. The same God who was a refuge and help to you this past year is ready to be the same to you and me this coming year.

So, let's get busy.